Forsaken Tales

Ali Fadel

DEDICATION

Here you are, dear reader

Contents

ACKNOWLEDGMENTS

To all friends

The Horror of the Marshes

Welcome to the marshes of gebayish. This is a story that may seem weirder than imaginationn. And it is stranger than imagination... But I don't care whether you believe the story or not. But it happened. One cold winter day, when the sun started to rise, at five o'clock in the morning. I went to mashkhov. Birds were chirping happily. And the atmosphere was calm as usual early in the morning. I went up on a mashkhov back. With a spear and a net. Of course, I forgot to tell you that fishing is my livelihood and the livelihood of many families here. With the cultivation and raising of buffaloes. I didn't know at that time that my life would change from a quiet and simple one to one of horror and full of nightmares at night.

The strangest thing that happened that day, as far as I remember, was the presence of that strange corpse that appeared on the surface. I rowed the mashkhov deep into the marshes. I threw a net into water that was a meter and a half deep. And waited for my livelihood to come. The sun was jumping little by little. As if she were a child growing slowly. Meanwhile ... Breathe in clean air. I forgot to tell you. The air is fresh, comfortable, and clean. Free of pollutants like smoke from cars and factories, as in the city, I heard a movement behind me. I turned around and saw a herd of black buffaloes passing by me as they swam, and I couldn't see anything of them except their big heads coming out of the water.

Buffaloes moved away to graze in a place far from me and during that... I saw something that caught my interest. Bubbles ... Strange bubbles started to come out of the water near me. I was surprised at the beginning of something. I have never seen anything like this before.

"abu haidar, good morning."

I heard a familiar voice from a distance. I looked at the source of the sound. And I saw Razzaq rowing with the boat...

Approaching me, "good morning,"

Razzaq approached my makhshoof and said, "How is the situation with you?".

"normal ".

Razak replied with a laugh: "I told you to go out two or three hours before dawn; you won't find any fish now."

"I don't like the night!"

Razzaq laughed. "Why? Are you afraid of tantal?! ".

Razzaq's laughter rose loudly; he smiled in my turn courtesy of my friend's joke, and Razzaq cut off his laughter when he saw bubbles.

"What is this, abu haidar?".

I looked at the bubbles that were close to us, and i said to my companion,

"I don't know, this is the first time I've seen this thing!"

"let's see it; maybe there's a dead animal here or a turtle stuck in the water."

Razzaq moved towards the bubbles until he reached them. Razzaq raised his spear, with which he usually fishes, and began to hit the bubble. Here Razzaq shouted towards me: "abu haidar, come quickly."

I moved my mashkhov, saying, "what?".

"Something here; do you see it?".

I looked at the sides of the bubbles.

So, I saw something...

Something white...

I lifted my spear from a scary roof.

Then I said to Razzaq, "what is this thing?".

"don't ask me; I don't know."

We started hitting him here and Razzaq together with the two spears. And here... Something happened...

The thing appeared from under the water. And he started to float in front of our eyes. The blood froze in our veins at that moment, and that's where we saw that thing. Wrapped in a white shroud, it was a corpse, for whom? We don't know. "Look, it's chained!"

Said Razzaq as he knelt on the back of his mashkhov., trying to drag a body towards him. I said to Razzaq as I swallow my saliva, "who killed her? And why is she chained?"

The thing that made me surprised—and Razzaq is also surprised—is the chains tied to the corpse. They were thick chains. Wrapped around the corpse.

"abu haidar, come help me!"

Razzaq pulled a body towards his boat, so I jumped from my boat to his boat. And we pulled the body from the marsh water. The first thing i felt when I pulled the body was. Was the weight of the body. It was strangely heavy. Although Razzaq was with me, I felt like I was pulling something heavier than me. We put the body of al-bayda wrapped on the deck of the Razzaq boat. I got up from my place and asked Razzaq, "where do we go with it?".

Razzaq replied, looking at something strange:

"Look, what are these letters and signs?!".

I looked at the canvas of a corpse or shroud, and here I saw... Red marks, words, and letters... I've never seen anything like it in my life.

I looked at the canvas of a corpse or shroud, and here I saw... Red marks, words, and letters...

I've never seen anything like it in my life. I quickly told Razzaq,

"Let's take it to Hajji Hussein."

But Razzaq didn't look at me like he didn't hear my words. His being was stunned by that corpse.

Like a thief who saw a precious jewel. I said to Razzaq,

"Razzaq, let's go to Hajji Hussein."

I returned to my boat, and Razzaq moved his boat quickly... Heading to Haji Hussein's house. And within minutes, we came out from the depths of the marshes. We arrived at Haji Hussein's house.

And the house made of sugarcane rose high. And from outside the house, wooden walls surrounded the remote island. As you know, the people of the marshes live on small islands.

We arrived at the entrance of the house. And Razzaq went up to a hill, shouting at Haji Hussein. While I kept waiting for him. And in seconds, Razzaq returned with the great sheik.

Haji Hussein. He is sixty years old. Haji Hussein, who was walking on his crutches, approached and looked at me,

Then looked inside a boat, and his eyes widened in horror and panic. Haji Husayn said,

"What is this corpse?".

Razak quickly replied, "I suddenly floated on the surface of the water."

Haji Hussain looked into tired eyes at me and said, "Abu Haidar, where did you find this corpse?".

I explained, "Deep inside the marshes, the place where we usually catch fish."

Haji Hussain touched his long beard with long fingers, saying,

"Strange, I've never seen anything like this in my life."

"Look at these chains and locks!" said Razzaq with clear anxiousness.

The three of us looked; the thick chains were tied around a corpse with tights, and there were seven large locks as if they had been made especially for this corpse!!...

Razzaq said, "What shall we do with it, O Sheikh?".

The great sheikh replied with a clear tone of concern: "Return it to water; And only care about your affairs!"

Razak replied: "What if it is someone's body? We have to call the police."

"Zaraq's words are true; what if it was the body of someone?"

Haji Hussein smiled, saying: "Even if it is a corpse, its owner is gone, and you know if the police come,

They will wreak havoc on the village and disturb our mood."

You may be surprised by Haji Hussein's words. But the truth is that our relationship with the government as Marsh residents is like the relationship of the dead with the living...

We don't want any connection with the government. Especially since Haji Hussein has had a blind hatred of the government since the time of the Baathist regime in Iraq.

And you know...

Some wounds are better buried in the depths. Haji Hussain quickly said,

"Take the body and put it back in place."

Razak replied by asking, "Do you expect Haji Hussain that a body will return? You know...Honor killing?!".

Haji Hussain wiped his beard and leaned on his crutch with a clear heaviness as he said,

"I can't imagine that, even if this is a corpse. Honor killing of... So why tie them with chains and iron locks?".

Razzaq looked at me, and I looked at him in my turn.

Haji Hussain hurriedly said, "Go before one of you sees you, and this is a story that will not come out of anyone's mouth."

"As Haji Hussain wishes,"

Razzaq and I left and went back to the place where we found the body.

Pushing the body from a roof that is scared, Razzaq said,

"It belongs to Allah, and Him, we shall return."

After we finished our work, Razzaq left with obvious signs of anxiety, and I, in turn, left for a second spot to fish after the sun rose above my head. And I thought the horror was over here...

But this is just the beginning of more terrifying events that happened in our village. In Morocco, I sat outside a house made of sugarcane, mud, and straw. I sat outside on a carpet in the Nerve tranquilizer air.

Above my head, the stars shine like lamps. And the sounds of frogs spread around me.

I sat smoking cigarette after cigarette to eliminate the boredom of the daily routine of life.

To hear something from inside my house. Freezing blood in my veins.

I heard a noise inside my house.

Sensation...

The strange thing...

I did not tell you that I live alone. An old man. I am 54 years old. Death kidnapped my wife three years ago...

And God didn't give me offspring. After me, and this is something that makes me sad and desperate.

Especially if I reached the age of gray hair, I would not reach that age, and I could not get married again or have children.

I got up to check on the noise that had happened in my house.

I carried the fire lantern and left, moving with heavy and slow steps toward my wooden door.

I opened the door. To be surprised by something, make the fire lantern fall from my hands in horror.

She's back.

I opened the door. To be surprised by something, make the fire lantern fall from my hands in horror.

"In the name of Allah, the Most Gracious, the Most Merciful, I seek refuge in Allah from the evil of the dreaded Satan."

In the center of the room, my bed, she lay...

The corpse...

With its white shroud and its thick chains. And its iron locks, one of which weighs More than my weight! At that time, I smelled a strange perfume. Very strange. In front of my eyes, I swear to God. The body moved!! ...

I screamed in horror as I stepped backward.

"I seek refuge in Allah; I seek refuge in Allah; I seek refuge in Allah; in the name of Allah, the Merciful, I seek refuge in Allah."

And I backed out of my house. And I walked with all the strength I had in my weak body. And I was scared, looking at my house in horror. Leaving the door open and the lantern thrown on the ground. I rowed My boat... In the middle of darkness, In the middle of the marshes, where? To Razzaq's house, of course. Luckily for me, Razzaq's house was not far from me. I parked my boat scaredly and went up to an island, crossing wooden fences and the flags of the red and black Razak clan fluttering over the grizzly hair. I knocked on Razzaq's house door violently. "Razzaq! Razzaq!! ".

Razzaq opened the door, wiping his eyes from sleepiness. The inhabitants of the marshes sleep at sunset, Razzaq said, wearing his white dishdasha, saying to me, "What's the matter, Abu Haidar?".

"The corpse! The corpse is in my house!"

Razzaq's eyes widened with indescribable terror. And swallowed my saliva. And behind Razzaq appeared his wife and four children. One of his eldest sons approached and said to his father,

"What's the matter, Dad? "

"Nothing; stay here,"

Razzaq said in a sharp tone to his son. I rode with Razzaq in my boat. While rowing me to my house, Razzaq asked me anxiously,

"How did the body return? We threw it into the water, right? "

"Right."

Razzaq asked me again, "Where did you find it? "

"In my bedroom, I swear to God she was moving!! ".

"Move?? "

" By Almighty God, I am not lying to you; you have moved in front of me."

We arrived at my house. Razzaq and I went up a hill and headed to my house. We found a lantern lying on the ground, and the door was wide open. Razzaq looked inside. His eyes widened in panic, and he swallowed as he repeated,

"In the name of Allah, the Most Gracious, the Most Merciful, I seek refuge in Allah from the evil of the accursed Shaytan."

The body was there! Razak approached and was braver than me. He carried a stick of sugarcane that was thrown on the floor of a room.

"She was moving; I swear to God, I saw her! "

Move Razzaq's body with the oud. A little...

I approached the door of my house. I expect to run away at any time. My weak heart can't stand such things. Strange corpses appear in your bedroom for no reason. I used to hear things like this in fairy tales. The body didn't move. In the name of Allah, the Most Gracious, the Most

Merciful, Razzaq said, moving a corpse again. Nothing happened. Razzaq said,

"How did a body come here? I don't know."

"Did anyone see us throwing the body into the water? "

Answer Razzaq's question: "No."

Razzaq and I went out of my house, and he said to me,

"How did this body come here? You want to tell me that a corpse came here alone?"

You don't believe me, Razak; I swear to God, I didn't bring the body here."

"Let's go to Haji Hussain and tell you the story."

"And a corpse, what do we do with it?"

"We'll bring it with us."

Thus, Razzaq and I carried the corpse together, and my nerves at the time were on the hottest of embers. If the corpse had moved at that time, my heart would have stopped in horror. We put the body on a boat and We rowed to the house of the great sheikh. We went up a hill and crossed the wooden walls of the Amer house. Leaving the body alone in a boat. Razzaq knocked on the door of the great sheikh. We heard a voice from inside saying, "Who is at the door? ".

"I am Razzaq, Haji Hussein."

"Open the door."

Razzaq opened the door, and the great Sheikh was lying on a bed of papyrus cane, and the smell of incense was strong in the place. Next to the sheikh was a basket of dates. And the sheikh was swimming while supporting his back against the wall. The big sheikh was surprised by my presence with Razzaq. The Shaykh said, "Excuse me, I cannot get up."

Razak replied, "No, our sheikh, we are sorry to bother you; we have come with an important matter."

The sheikh smiled and said to us, "Sit us in front of me."

Razzaq and I sat down, and the Shaykh presented us with a basket of dates in front of us, and he thanked us, saying, Haji Hussein, Abu Haidar will tell you the story. And I told the great sheikh the whole story, and the sheikh listened with clear interest, despite the signs of anxiety and astonishment that appeared on his facial features, which he tried to hide. After I finished telling my story, the great sheikh said, "Where is she now? ".

"We left her with the scarf outside."

"Well, pick up the corpse and put it in the host."

Razzaq and I went out together and went back to Mashkhov carrying the body heavily, to the point that I felt that my back would break at any moment. We entered the wide host. It could accommodate 40 people.

Made of yellow sugarcane. White fans used to spread the smell of incense all over the host. And the flag of Iraq was placed on the reed wall at the end of the session.

And on the sides of the host, the antique weapons were placed. And in the middle of the host.

It was a tea pot and a coffee with yellow colors...

The big ones and the small ones. On a burned wood stove. We put the body at the end of the host.

And the big sheikh entered us with his crutch and his prominently curved back.

"In the name of Allah, the Most Gracious, the Most Merciful,"

The sheikh said when he saw the body. Razzaq said to the Shaykh,

"What are you going to do with it? "

The sheikh replied, "In the morning, I want you and Razzaq to bring Abu Raad."

"ABO Raad? "Razzaq replied with astonishment.

I said here, "Sheikh, do you not mean that crazy person in our village?! "

Sheikh Kabir smiled, caressing his long beard. "Sometimes he knows madmen better than we do! "

We thanked the Sheikh, and we got out of the room. And I returned Razzaq to his house after the melodious night fell on our marshes.

The truth is that I was terrified of two things, which are...

The order to leave the body at Haji Hussein's. And secondly, it is my return to my house.

I feel a horror shaking my being from within. Something was telling me not to come back.

But I counted: I went into my house, put a fire lantern near a bed, and looked around inside the room looking for something...

Until I got sleepy and slept. In the middle of the night...I woke up to a strange sound. Something is inside the room with me!!...

Crazy in the middle of the night...

I woke up to a strange sound. Something is inside the room with me!!...

I opened my sleepy eyes and saw darkness hanging over me. I looked beside the bed; the fire lantern was extinguished.

Strange...

I remember filling the tank with oil. According to my experience. On a lamp to turn it off in the morning when I wake up. So, what turned off the flashlight next to my head?!

I heard a strange sound at the edges of the bed. "Who is there? ".

My voice reverberated throughout the dark room. No one answered me. But I still felt so scared, to the point of crying. At the end of the bed. Something is standing there. "In the name of Allah, the Most Gracious, the Most Merciful, seek refuge in Allah from the evil of the dreaded Satan,"

I spoke, repeating verses from the Holy Quran with a loud voice. I'm trying my best. To keep my mind intact and not let the darkness show me what I don't want to see. But at but at some point, an arm with long nails protruded beside the bed. I screamed in horror. And I see a bald head coming out slowly. And there were some long locks of hair here and there. The creature looked at me with yellow eyes. So, I screamed, and my weak heart almost stopped. I opened my eyes to discover that something was just a nightmare—a terrifying nightmare.

I looked at the fire lantern; it was lighting up the room with light that chased away all the darkness in the room. I felt a little comfortable looking around the room, and I couldn't find anything. At this moment, Cut the scary silence... Knocking on my door. Noisy high roads as if knocking... He knocks with both hands!

"Who is there? ".

The roads stopped in a moment of silence. I swallowed my saliva in horror. And my frail body started trembling because of anxiety. I wonder who is there... The night hasn't gone yet. So, who comes up with this late hour?

I went back knocking, and here I jumped out of bed, so terrified and anxious that with every step I heard my heartbeat... In every plan, as I head to a door, I am afraid that it is her. And who do you think? ...I opened the door of my house carrying a fire lantern, and I found no one! I looked to my right and to my left. There was no one... I shouted,

"Razzaq, Razzaq, get out; you scared me, man."

But no voice answered... Quiet was the master of the place. Even the sounds of frogs and cockroaches. We're not heard that night. As if there were mysterious forces that forced everyone to be silent. I wanted to close the door if I hadn't noticed something strange. There are dead birds at the door. The lantern brought the fire closer to the birds, which became clear to me.

They're crows! Crows!

How? There are no crows in the marshes!!...

As far as I know, crows prefer desert areas and countryside. There are no bodies of water like swamps. And I calculated their number. There were about 20 dead crows. Who killed them? Or a correct question here. Who brought them to my doorstep at night?!! ...

Close the door to my house. I jumped on a bed and covered you up to the bottom of my feet, and I was trembling with terror. I'm so scared I can't show my head and see the place around me. Lest I see what my little heart can't bear. The sun rose with its yellow light. Of course, I didn't sleep all night. My black thoughts were manipulating me, like a cat manipulating a mouse.

In the morning, I decided to go fishing; at least I wanted to go back to my normal routine. Fishing...

Sitting at night under the stars, smoking cigarettes, and sleeping without terrifying nightmares...

All these things I felt I missed...

Strongly, and the reason is obvious. That damn corpse...

Since I floated in water until my life became a circle of horrible nightmares, maybe you're wondering...

Is horror over here? ... Of course... Listen, what happened when I went fishing? And I wish I hadn't done...

Listen to what happened when I went fishing...

And I wish I hadn't done...

I went out to fish as usual at three in the morning. It was a shining day. The people of the village are sleeping quietly and peacefully. Of course, except for myself, I didn't sleep. As I told you...

I carried my belongings, represented by the spear and the white net. Then I went down to the water and rode my boat, which can barely accommodate two people, and then I began to row towards the depths of the marshes. Birds are flying over my head. And a herd of buffaloes passes by me. Also, some turtles swim next to my boat.

And the sky is clear with its blue color, and a cold wind hits your cheeks violently. Everything was perfect for a beautiful day.

But...

I stopped rowing. I threw the white net at a close distance from me., took out a pack of cigarettes from a dishdasha shirt and a lighter, and lit a cigarette in that cold weather in the morning.

Smoke will quietly come out of my mouth...

And close my eyes for a few seconds, trying to forget all that happened. Something moved the boat!

I almost fell.

I leaned on the surface of my fear and wondered what happened—what moved the boat so violently?... But I didn't care much. Sometimes... Turtles, known here as reefs, sometimes collide with boats while swimming in the water. Another violent tremor...

Well, maybe you were wrong in your explanation. Kick doesn't move a boat with this force and violence! I took a breath of cigarette smoke, trying to relax. And I gathered my courage to see around a boat. Fortunately, it was morning, because I didn't see it at that moment. He made me scream with goosebumps of horror. A cry from the bottom of my weak heart. When I stared into the water to see... What hits the boat so hard?...

I saw three human faces happening underwater!! ...

I screamed as I retreated to the back of my boat. Even a cigarette fell out of my arm. Oh God, what did you just see?...

Specters?

Tantal?

Lives?

"In the name of Allah, the Most Gracious, the Most Merciful, seek refuge in Allah from the evil of the dreaded Satan."

And I started repeating some verses of the Quran until the horror and fear disappeared from my heart. I don't know how an old heart can bear all this horror over the past three days. ...

"Good morning, Abu Haidar! "

That was Razzaq. Thank you, God. This bastard saved me. I shouted as I saw Razak approaching my Mashkhov:

"Razzaq, come quickly."

Mashkhov Razzaq stood next to my fear, and Razzaq went up on my boat. He was surprised by me while I was sleeping on my back, saying,

"I took Abu Haidar's nap! "

"Razzaq, do you see anything in the water? "

Razak raised his eyebrows in wonder, saying, "What do you mean? ".

"Look! Look at the water around my boat."

Razzaq looked around the boat, then furrowed his eyebrows and said,

"I don't understand; what do you mean? "

"Swear to God, I have seen human faces in the water! "

"Human faces! "By God Almighty,"

Razak laughed. "You're acting weird today; have you slept well? Your eyes—"

"I know, I know, I didn't sleep yesterday."

"Why? "Something was knocking on my door. And when I opened the door, I didn't find anyone! "

Razak raised his eyebrows, saying,

"Strange, the same thing happened to me!! "

Razzaq stood upright, and I looked into Razak's eyes and said,

"Really? "

"By God, yesterday someone was knocking on my door hard. My son Jassim opened the door, but he didn't find anyone, and my wife kept saying that she heard the sound of breaths near her head when he was sleeping! "

I swallowed my saliva from excessive terror. Something was breathing at your head while you slept.

This is my worst nightmare. Here Razzaq remembered something important:

"When do we go to Abu Raad's house?".

I remembered the words of Haji Hussein and how he told us yesterday that we have to bring Abu Raad to him, so I said, explaining,

"Noon, we will bring Abu Raad and come to Haji Hussein."

I decided at that time that I had enough fishing at that time. And to eat in Beit Razzaq because this is safer for me.

Maybe you feel like laughing at me because I'm a coward and I can't go home.

But honestly, I don't care about your opinion.

I'm old at the end.

And at any moment, the Lord takes his faithfulness.

And I don't want to live my last days in worry and horror about scary things and nightmares at night.

At noon...

Me and Razzaq decided to go to Abu Raad's house...

This was another nightmare waiting for us.

The cold winds were blowing with unprovoked force and violence.

However, there was some warmth and hope in the bright sunlight.

And we rowed together—me and Razzaq—in a direction far from the marshes. Because Abu Raad was always a person who preferred to mix with himself rather than make contact with others.

And the walls made of reeds surrounded the hill.

Therefore, you can't see Abu Raad's house except when you enter through a door and cross the walls of Alkasabiya.

He believes in myths and old tales. And he doesn't have a circle of relationships.

Few people who know Abu Raad.

And very few love him. Or are comfortable when he is near them.

Abu Raad's house was made of straw and mud—a quiet, silent, and suspicious house at the same time.

But as soon as we got home,

We saw...

The strangest thing we have seen in our lives...

Razzaq knocked on the door several times. But we didn't hear a voice inside.

And more worrying is that the atmosphere surrounding this house is suspicious and uncomfortable.

Even the air feels its weight when you pass the walls of the yellow bronchi.

A mysterious house as its owner, even herds of buffaloes.

Although they graze everywhere in marshes and approach every house. Except.

The house of our friend Abu Raad Buffaloes was afraid this was a house.

Or maybe you are afraid, which is not an appropriate word here...

She was afraid...

Buffaloes were afraid of this house and everything that surrounded it.

Even birds...

Since the sun is prominent, you see birds flying everywhere over all houses, except this house.

"Abu Raad, Abu Raad! "

Razzaq shouted more than once, but no answer came to us.

Razzaq looked at me and said, "What are we going to do?".

And an answer almost came out of my mouth...

If it weren't for the wooden door...

He opened wide on his own!!

Razzaq and I heard the creak of the terrifying door opening in front of us, and there was no one behind him. We looked inside; there was no one in the house. Razzaq said, "Let's check out a house that may have hit Abu Raad."

In fact, I wished we had left this house. Mysterious forces surround this house. It makes me feel a kind of discomfort. We got inside. The room was tidy but strange. When you get inside...

You see a bed placed to your right. And there you are on your left. A carpet is furnished on the floor, and on it are yellow jugs. And next to it was an incense burner that was spreading incense that smelled strange, or, to be honest, strongly smelly, and right in front of you.

A wooden statue in the shape of a human sitting on a throne. But with a goat's head. The statue was large. It's the size of a room's bed!

And I forgot to tell you that next to the yellow jugs...

Some books were clear from their yellow papers that they were old. Very old.

Even the ink on which the words are written has dried up over time to the extent that some words have become illegible. How does this man read?

"What is this statue, Abu Haidar? "

Razzaq asked me. "I don't know." And here I looked at the ceiling and found...

Some dead birds coming down from the roof by spider threads. Many birds of different colors and shapes. Even some birds. I'm sure... Some birds don't live in our marshes. Where did this man get it from?

"What do you want?".

We heard a strange voice behind us. Razzaq and I turned at the same moment. And here we saw Satan himself. The corpse is huge. Its length is equivalent to two meters. Its hair is long to the shoulders, and the color of the night is black. A face that is congenitally distorted to the extent that one look is enough to terrify your heart. And she was wearing a white dishdasha, dirty with mud. And there are spots. That looks like...

Clotted blood resembles.

There and there in different places.

I swallowed my saliva as I saw him entering from his house door.

Abu Ra'Ad, "how are you? "

"Fine," Abu Raad replied in a sharp, dry tone.

"What do you want? "We asked in a hostile frenzy as if to say that we are not welcome here.

"Haji Hussain wants to see you," Razzaq replied,

And here you notice the amount of worry and terror in Razzaq's tone of voice.

He didn't even blink for a moment.

Abu Raad walked with his huge body towards his old books and bent down to close them.

Then he got up, standing without turning to us.

"What does the Sheikh want? "

He wants to see you about something.

" Abu Ra'ad turned around and turned my gaze away from the disfigured face, and Abu Ra'd said quickly,

"What's up? "

Razak breathed and said,

"We found a body in the water! "

Abu Raad said in an exclamatory tone, "Abu Haidar and I found her in the water three days ago."

I am sure that Abu Raad looked at me, but I was busy looking at ants on the ground.

At least ants are easier than the face of the devil. I felt Abu Raad's gaze watching me, and after a moment of silence, he told us,

"What have you done to them? "

"We put it at Haji Hussain, and now he wants you."

A moment of silence came again, and Abu Raad said, "Why didn't you call the police at that time? "

"The sheikh advised us not to call... Because the corpse... Was a strange corpse."

"Strange? How? "

"Wrapped in a white shroud and tied with large chains and seven locks."

"What! "

Abu Raad screamed; his scream shook the house and almost fell over our heads.

Even the blood inside my nerves has frozen from excessive fear.

Abu Ra'ad said as he walked out of the door of his house, "Come with me quickly."

Razzaq and I followed him, and Razzaq asked him,

"What is the matter? Why?". Abu Raad interrupted him, saying,

You have brought calamities over our heads. "We have to hurry to the house of the sheikh."

Asked Razzaq, and I could barely keep up with them towards Mashkhov.

Abu Raad stopped as he turned to us and said, "Sheikh... Sheikh Hussein is in great danger..."

We arrived at the house of Sheikh Hussein...

Abu Raad went down in front of us, and Razzaq and I were behind them. And we walked to Haji Hussein's house.

And Abu Raad knocked several noisy roads from the palm of his huge hand.

But there was no sound.

Anxiety started to flow between my ribs like a black disease.

Razak said, "We'll see him in a host, maybe."

The three of us were deported, but we didn't find anyone in the host, nor a corpse either.

So, Abu Raad said to us,

"Where is the corpse? Where is she? "

"We don't know! ".

Razzaq replied with a clear note of concern. And here we heard a voice outside a host.

A strange sound.

We came out of the house to find someone in front of us.

Sheikh Hussein. But he was not the Sheikh Hussein we know.

His face has been completely disfigured. His eyes are red, like the colour of fire. His teeth are covered with blood.

He has a barren body and is wearing only his underwear.

He crawls. He crawls on all four limbs!! He looked at us.

Sheikh Hussein.

He was not a human.

I repeat, he never looked like a human.

"What is this?! "Said Razzaq in a questioning tone.

The monster emitted a strange snarl and moved quickly on its four limbs, like a three-footed beast.

And he pounced on Razzaq because he was closer to him.

And the beast started biting Razzaq. Until blood was shed on his clothes.

Abu Raad turned behind the beast and carried it back, shouting at him,

"Take your friend and run! "

I stood stunned in front of a scene...

Frozen...

I can't face these events. "Run, run."

I moved towards Razzaq, and here I saw the bite of the monster with sharp fangs.

I helped Razzaq rise with all the strength I had in my body.

While ABO Raad and the beast are fighting and I and Razzaq Al-Muadhd are moving towards the walls of a house, I only felt the monster swooping on me from behind. I fell on my face.

And on my back, the monster grabbed my neck and bit me.

I felt his sharp fangs piercing my flesh.

I screamed.

I screamed with all my voice. I screamed.

At this moment.

Abu Raad hit the monster to keep him away from me, and indeed, he hit him with a fishing spear in the head.

The spear pierced the head of the beast. The monster fell off my back. And I started to writhe on the soil.

I swear to God, I heard a voice. The bones of the beast were breaking—yes, breaking.

And he makes involuntary movements. And here I consciously lost sight...

In a dream, I was walking slowly, carrying a torch—a torch of fire. I don't know how I got it or where I am....

In a long corridor...

Dark and cold. And at the end... Spacious room.

It was very wide as if it were a temple. And in front of you stands...

A group of strangers...

Because of the distance, I can't see their features and faces.

But they were wearing black completely from head to toe.

Standing in two rows. A row from the right and a row from the left, a staircase goes up...

I don't know where...

But I couldn't control my body.

And I felt that there are forces greater than me that control my weak body.

I went up one step after another to what looked like the altar. And there she was. Lying on a shrine... And the light falls on it from a crystal hanging from the ceiling. Her skin is as white as ice. Her whole body was tattooed, from neck to foot. She had four arms... In each hand, you have six fingers. And on her right chest and left, two human faces settle from the ugliest faces... One of them is for an ugly princess. And another face was for a man who is worse than a woman. Her lips were black like coal. She had her eyes closed.

And in the next moment...

She opened her eyes in a breathtaking moment. I had a chance until my voice was torn. I woke up from my coma to find myself in someone's house. And there was a man next to me. The man's eyes settled, making it clear to me. He is a Marshes resident, and his name is Jasem. He said while playing with his scarves,

"Are you okay, brother?"

"Where am I?"

I asked Jasem. "In my house, Abu Raad told me what happened."

Remember something important here...

And I said, "Razzaq! Rice!"

Jassim interrupted me and said, "Razzaq is fine; we sent Abu Ahmad to him."

Abu Ahmed is the only doctor in the marshes. He was serving in the Iraqi army during the U.S. invasion of Iraq in 2003. I felt a strong headache and indescribable dizziness. I tried to get up because my body let me down, and I breathed loudly. Jassim said to me,

"Why did you kill Sheikh Hussein?! "

I looked at Jasim and said, "What? "

"You have been killed, Sheikh Hussein."

"Nope, I have; I've"

"Called the police; they will come tomorrow, and you and Razzaq and Abu Raad will get your punishment."

"Jassim, you—"shshut u up, murderer!"

He yelled at me, his tone of voice turning from calm to outrage.

Jasim got up from the side of the bed and then went out of his house.

And I heard him talking to someone outside: "Watch him well; if he tries to escape, hit him."

At that time, he gave in to despair and sadness. Sheikh Hussein died and how will we convince everyone of what happened?

I left for a dream world because of the pain in my neck.

I woke up again to another nightmare!

I left for a dream world because of the pain in my neck. I woke up again to another nightmare. I heard a noise outside the house where I was sleeping. Loud noise. It's like there's a fight outside. I panicked, and the drums of my heart started beating violently. I got up from bed slowly. Feeling dizzy and tired, I walked to the wooden door, and I opened it a little so I could see. Nothing. There was no one.

So, what is this noise that you heard? ... I opened the door wide and made that annoying and terrifying sound at the same time. And I went out of the house barefoot. I looked around me; there was no one nearby, no guards, no Jasem. A calm situation. But calm like this is what terrified my heart. The suspicious calm of the nerves.

At this moment, I saw something in the darkness in front of me. It looked like fire lamps, but it was far away. I approached this thing, and it was located directly behind the walls of the house. I got closer and closer. I have a deadly curiosity about logic. The sensations were flowing like rivers inside my soul. And when I reached the walls of a house, I saw. It was floating in the air. I swear to God. You don't believe me. But I swear the body was floating in the air in front of me, and it wasn't a lying position, but it was erect. And what was around her was more terrifying than her tens and tens.

Corpses ...

Some of them, I know. And some others, no. They were Marsh residents!! ... Hanging in the air. The bodies rotate in a circle around their lady. And in the next moment...

Yellow eyes shone from behind the white shroud. I screamed in terror as I ran back to a house behind me. I closed the door. And I am repeating all the verses of the Quran that I knew in my life when I heard her voice.

It's coming!

I stepped back from the door, and my eyes didn't blink for a moment. The door opened wide with unbelievable force, to the extent that it was taken out of its place. And the crows got inside. I knelt, screaming in horror.

That they are around me—all of them. Crows and dead bodies. I saw them standing in a room with me. Standing with white eyes protruding,

Lifeless ... Seeing them alone was enough to terrify the bravest hearts. Ending it... While kneeling on a room carpet and they were around me, I heard her footsteps approaching me. At every step, A heart was beating its drums as hard as it could. I saw her feet at the beginning. White as snow and long nails like monsters. I felt a mysterious force lift my head. So that...

To see her. And when I looked at those yellow eyes radiating like fire, I had all the feelings at that time:

Fear.

Anger.

Horror.

Anxiety.

Peace.

Quiet.

Everything was comfortable in those eyes.

It's her. She's the God I hoped would come. I don't remember anything except that I looked into those eyes for many eons, even whole centuries. Life, death, space, time, and everything else. Understandable and incomprehensible. Inside those yellow eyes were...

I'm free to... I've finally been liberated.

You've been liberated from everything. I feel at peace with myself, with my soul, mind, and body, and with everything in this vast universe. At the end, I saw a light yellow. A yellow light flooded everything—my soul, my mind, even my body—to which I surrendered without my will. Rest and peace together. How beautiful they are! Maybe you're wondering at this moment. What happened after that? Let me finish for you.

Since we've reached the end of my story, I woke up in the morning. Everything was peaceful. I felt like I could do anything as if I were born again. A young man full of unparalleled strength and energy.

I rowed to the house of the people of the marshes. And let me tell you why I did that. I know. Did they feel liberated like me? And indeed... They have been liberated. We have turned into higher and superior entities. Of human beings. Our bodies have turned blue. And we can breathe underwater. We don't need fishing. Because we are immortal. And we won't be affected by time anymore. What a life I wanted! Our fins are coming out of our backs. And our fingers merged to become three fingers instead of five. Maybe you are wondering. How could you bear all this? No, maybe you won't believe me, but it's true.

I didn't feel any pain. I felt comfortable and at peace. You're free now. We have speed and strength, so what do we need after this? Liberation... Our nostrils liberated us from the burden of breathing your dirty air, and our bodies are immortal and not affected by the omnipotent time for you. And we became free from our thoughts and feelings. We became one. We and her. Our lady...

What a great blessing it is to serve forces greater than hers! Maybe you are wondering what happened. Barzaq and Abu Raad. So, I did not forget them; Razzaq and his family were liberated too. As for Abu Raad, I found him hanging in his room while his eyes were kneeling with white, and his pale skin indicated that he saw what his mind could not bear.

You may be wondering why I am telling you this story... I don't know the answer to this question, but I invite you to become and serve the forces that control this universe, forces bigger than you and me and bigger than all other beings. Now, I'm gone forever, and you'll never see me again. And if you see it again...

Something comes out of the water.

So, no... You interfere with him and show him as if you never saw him. This is how you will live the rest of your days in peace.

Done.

Brother of Moon

As far as I know, the real horror started in December, that is, in the winter, and by the way, the whole town was covered in snow. Let me introduce myself to you. I'm Jack Smith, and I live in Norn town, in the north of Black Damon.

And by the way, it is one of the coldest places on this planet, where the temperature reaches 72 degrees below zero. This is talk in the winter. In summer, the temperature reaches only twenty degrees!

It was a night. Snow is falling very slowly. I was standing in front of the window with a glass of cold drink in my hand while soft music emanated from the radio subject in the corner of the room.

"Jack... Stop looking out the window. Someone will see you!"

Maybe you are surprised by the words of... But let me tell you, this is a town. Norn town. It is forbidden to drink or sell alcohol, so I was in the barrel of the cannon in case someone saw me drink a glass of cold wine.

I told her:

"Sarah, my love. Don't worry, everything is fine."

But Sarah replied:

Enough sarcasm... You were arrested last week. Don't forget that."

This is my wife. Sarah Kudman... She is thirty-five years old, while I am thirty-six years old. She has blond hair, while I have black hair. She has green eyes, while I have brown eyes. And that's how I described myself and my wife to you.

Any way... Sarah said to me, putting dinner plates on a table:

"Jack, dinner is ready."

She quickly drank the drink and then sat down in front of her, saying,

"The smell of food is indescribable."

Sarah smiled gently, saying,

"Let's eat."

And the moments pass one after another. Like a train loaded with trailers. It passes through a dark tunnel.

Pass one trailer after another. And so on, after half an hour.

I took the dishes off the table, and I sat smoking a cigarette and looking at the ceiling of the room.

But it was only a short moment until my wife came back from the kitchen.

She stood by me. I paid attention to her. I found signs of anxiety painted on her face, and ten years after we were married, I knew what she was thinking. And what do you think?

I told her:

"Sarah ... There's something you're hiding from me, right?"

She started playing with her hair tresses, and this is a movement that, if it indicates tension and anxiety, I went back and asked her:

"What's up? Tell me?"

Sarah sat at a table in front of me, avoiding looking into my eyes.

I told her:

"Is it about procreation?"

FYI Although we have been married for nearly six years, we have not even had a single child. And let me give you an additional piece of information. There were whole nights we fought—me and her—over who was wrong in this matter.

But Jawab surprised me as she said:

"It's about something else, Jack."

And here I felt fear and terror, and my brow began to sweat even though the room was warm, so I said to her quickly:

"Sarah... Tell me. I'm starting to worry."

"I... I'm pregnant!"

My eyes widened to the point that they almost came out of their skull, and I got up from a chair, screaming:

" Really. What are you saying? Is this just a lie? Swear to me."

She got up with tears in her eyes, saying,

"I swear to you. It's a fact."

Here, an adult voice rang out on my device. So, I rushed to him.

A communiqué is coming from Miller's house. Neighbors reported hearing loud fights, and of course, who doesn't know Miller's family consists of a father named Henry and a wife named Mary, and of course they don't have any children?

I got out of my car, then went up the stairs of the house and knocked on the door.

The sky was pitch black. And the snow covers everything around you. You only see a white color, and anyway, the Miller family house had two floors, and like most houses in Norn town,

I opened the door, Mary. I noticed a blue bruise on her right eye. And of course, she raised a bottle of drink at me, saying:

"Go ahead, Jack."

I went inside the house. I found Henry to be a very fat man. And a bald head and eyes like pigs' eyes. As for his clothes, they are almost torn from obesity. How does this pig live?

He was standing near the dining table and looking at me with those piggy-brown eyes.

I put my hand on my gun, saying,

"Henry, you know the rules here. I arrested you three times last week."

He interrupted me as saliva poured out of his mouth, saying,

"I didn't do anything wrong... I love whiskey."

I tried to calm him down, saying:

"Henry, you know the laws."

"Fuck you, Jack."

"Don't force me to do something bad. Get down on your knees and put your hands on your head."

In reality, the issue of shackling this Foolish is a task that is almost as serious. The danger of shackling a pig! If you understand what I mean, this is the body of the full one who almost swore that if he fell on you from above, he would make dough out of you on the ground.

Luckily. Henry was kind-hearted. And understanding. So, I arrested him and took him to an office to put him behind bars.

But the real horror started when he sat in front of me at a table. My colleague at work, Sofia, is also a policewoman.

I was smoking while I was looking out a window outside. She sat in front of me, and she was looking at me.

I told her:

"What's up? Tell me."

And let me tell you about Sofia. She's older than me here. Sofia lived her life here while I was here three months ago. Sofia is 35 years old. And She has red hair. And hazel eyes and let me tell you a secret about it. She always spies on people. Yes, she spies on people. And it's literally. She knows every small and big thing in every house in town.

Sophia told me:

"Have you noticed something strange in a town?"

I looked at her and then blew smoke into the air and said,

"What do you mean?"

Sophia looked into my eyes and said,

"It's been about two months since you've been here."

I interrupted her to correct her information.

"Three months."

"Well. Three months. And you didn't notice anything strange in this town? It's terrifying!"

She blew smoke, saying:

"No, I didn't see anything strange here. Except for the snow and the harsh cold."

"And yet?"

"I didn't see anything suspicious here. People are simple. We are almost isolated from the outside world, and what do you mean by you?"

Sophia breathed audibly as she said,

"People! Haven't you realized anything yet?"

I raised my shoulders indifferently, saying,

"What is wrong with people? If you mean that people behave strangely, then it is up to people, specifically due to the cold weather here. No one can afford this cold."

But her answer shocked me:

"It's not their behavior; it's something worse."

"Something worse?! I don't understand yet."

"Something evil surrounds this town... Something that makes... It makes people sterile."

And while snow hit my car glass, I was coming back from a sheriff's office. I was recalling what Sofia said about the people here. How come I didn't pay attention to this?

Since I set foot, this is a town. Three months ago, I didn't see a single child!! But over time and because of the many events that you meet in your life, it makes you forget a lot of things.

Halfway through, I got a phone call from someone, and I said,

"Jack is with you."

A sharp voice came to me, saying:

"Jack, I'm Michael. I think you need to see this."

"See what?"

"Something strange."

"Where is your location?"

"At the entrance to the forest specifically."

"Well. Wait for me there, and don't move."

"I'm waiting for you."

At the entrance to the woods, I found Michael. Let me tell you about it. He's a hunter who carries a hunting rifle with him and smokes heavily. And he wears black glasses. He has blue eyes and a red beard. He has a scar on his left cheek that he took as a souvenir from one of the wolves that attacked him while he was hunting a wild deer. Luckily for him, His limbs were completely spared, except for the scar representing the wolf's claws.

Michael said as he blew smoke:

"Jack ... How are you?"

"I'd rather get to the heart of a topic, as you know."

Michael laughed and blew smoke: "I'm not surprised at you; you're a capital boy, anyway. There's something I discovered yesterday that you have to see."

The cold winds were hitting my face. And I try hard to follow Michael's steps in the snow. But it's impossible to walk comfortably in this thick snow. When you run over it, it feels like a foot is slipping into a deep world. Very deep!

I said to Michael as I followed him:

"When do we get somewhere?"

And I got an answer quickly:

"We've already arrived."

And in front of us was a dark and wide cave. I looked at Michael, saying,

That's what you wanted to show me. "Cave "

"It's not a cave, sir. But what's inside it?"

Michael lit a red candle to illuminate the place and started to advance me. I was walking with my hand on my gun, just in case. On the other hand, I was carrying a torch.

Michael Lee said:

"Do you smell that, Jack?"

I smelled the atmosphere. Indeed, there is a smell. It has a bad smell, and it is a sulfur smell.

I said to Michael:

"The smell of sulfur. What's wrong with it?"

Michael Lee said:

"There's something you have to see. Come on."

As we walked down the dark corridor of the cave, I heard laughter. I quickly told Michael:

"Do you hear this? The sound of children's laughter!!".

"Nope. Maybe it's just an illusion. Come on."

And here we have reached an exciting part of the story. But Michael turned around and said to me,

"Look at this."

There were strange things on both sides of the cave. Petrified things, or... With the phrase more correct, it was petrified!

And there are, like, wooden poles coming out of the chests of some things.

I said to Michael as I pointed the torch at one of the things:

"What is this a joke?! I traveled every distance to see statues."

"Not statues... Look well!"

Here, I aimed a torch accurately. And I got closer to those things. And I realized that these are not statues:

"That's...".

"Corpses! These are bodies that have been fossilized."

I looked at Michael with my eyes wide.

"This doesn't make sense. Who did this?"

Michael's response:

"I don't know. But there's something strange about these corpses. Look well."

And I realized what Michael was aiming at, and I said:

"These are pegs."

Michael smoked a cigarette, saying:

"To whom do you think they put pegs? In a place of heart."

Because of my lack of knowledge, I asked Michael:

"I don't understand. What do you mean by that?"

Michael blew smoke, saying:

"These are corpses. The correct statement is not human."

"Not human?!"

"This is vampire corpses."

We went back to the entrance of the jungle. I sat in the driver's seat, and Michael approached me and asked me:

"What are you going to do about this cave?"

I looked at him and then said,

"I don't know. Anyway, let's –".

But he quickly interrupted me, saying,

"Have you heard of Dracul's cult, Jack?"

I raised my eyebrows and asked,

"Dracul's sect?! No, I haven't heard anything about it, and I don't want to hear about it."

Michael blew a cigarette and said,

"It is a sect that worships an evil entity. It is said that he dwells on the moon! And scary about the subject that they are among us here... In this damn town."

She smiled at Michael, saying,

"And where is the problem with that? Some people want to worship a God of their own."

"A real problem. Are the gossip that spreads about them."

"What kind of gossip, Michael?"

"They are said to be the reason why all the people in this town are sterile!!".

I was surprised by Michael's answer, and I told him:

"You know about it?"

"The only person who doesn't know is you, Jack. And I'm not surprised that you didn't pay attention to this because you're a new person in town."

"Well... The time for talking is over. If anything happens, call me."

"Concept."

I sat on a bed reading a horror novel called (The Beast). While Sarah was lying next to me.

I realized Sara was looking at me with her green eyes. I told her:

"What's up?"

"Did you know? I had a strong headache, so I went to Ludwig's family house to ask them for a headache remedy."

I interrupted her as I looked at the pages of the novel.

"Why did you go? There are medicines in the bathroom."

"They're all out of it. I have a severe headache these days."

And here a moment of silence came. So, I cut it off, saying,

"And what happened after you went to Charles's house?"

I got to know them. Rebecca's wife called me; she was a nice person, and her husband, Charles, was a dark man. I couldn't leave their house quickly. She invited me to have a cake.

I interrupted her, and I was annoyed by all this nonsense.

"Go to sleep."

"Stop reading. I'm talking to you, Jack."

I was more annoyed, but I decided to leave a novel, and then I looked at her green eyes, saying:

"Well... Let me tell you. You know me. If there's something important, get it into the heart of a topic without twisting and turning."

"Don't be mad at me, Jack. I was trying to draw details for you."

Please. Sarah. "Tell me something I want to hear."

Here, Sarah told me something strange:

"Did you know that they can't have children? It's been thirty years since they got married, and they didn't have any children."

And here I wanted to hear more information from her, so I said:

"Did you see anything strange or suspicious in their house?"

"Yes. Three strange things."

And here my eyes widened, and I asked her, saying:

"Three things? What do you mean?"

Sarah replied:

"Like, there aren't any mirrors in their house."

And here my eyes widened, and I asked her, saying:

"Three things? What do you mean by you?"

Sarah replied:

"Like there is no mirror in their house!"

I raised my eyebrows, asking:

"Unbelievable! A whole house without a mirror?"

Sarah nodded in agreement.

I moderated my sitting and then put my hand on my chin as I asked her:

"What's next?"

Sarah moderated as well and replied:

"And the second thing... They're all weird skin colors."

Here I realized what she was aiming for, and I said to her:

"Their skin color is pale, isn't it?"

Sarah raised her eyebrows in apparent stupidity and said,

"Yes. How do you know that?".

"It doesn't matter. Tell me the third thing you saw."

Here, Sarah replied:

"They don't have any crosses, and that's weird?"

Here I wondered:

"Maybe they're atheists for this reason."

Sarah interrupted me, saying:

"I asked a husband, and he told me they were Christians."

Here, I could see ice gathering on the transparent window glass. And a moment of silence came when I was thinking about myself. The bodies that I saw this morning in a cave with Michael. Don't leave my mind. Carcasses of vampires.

That's the only place where vampires and werewolves live. Horror stories

As far as we know, it doesn't happen in real life.

And so, I told Sarah to go to sleep. And I turned off the lamp so that the room would be dark.

"Jaaaaaak!" The sound of a scream resounded, which took me from a dream world to reality. I got up from bed and saw Sarah missing, so I pulled a staircase next to me, took a gun, and went down from the staircase to the first floor.

Sarah! Sarah!"

"Jack, Jack, I'm here!"

It was a voice coming from a kitchen, so I went to it, and here I saw Sarah kneeling on the ground crying while a man was wearing a black mask with cleft eyes and a mouth like those of bank robbers.

He was putting his gun on Sarah's head, equipped. I raised my gun at him and said in a threatening tone:

"Leave Sarah! And put down your weapon."

The man looked at me and then said in a very quiet voice:

"I think you see the fate of what awaits your wife if you don't let go of your gun."

I couldn't think of anything at that time. Then I dropped a gun on the ground.

"Throw it away."

The man said it quietly as if he had carried out operations like these dozens of times before.

I threw my gun and hit one of the legs of a table, then I got up and said,

"Who are you? And what do you want?"

The man said quietly:

"They paid me to bring your wife to them."

I raised my eyebrows, saying:

"They paid? Who are they?"

"It's none of your business."

Here I asked the man an important question:

"I'm not a murderer, right?"

The man's gaze was as cold as frost, and a man answered me:

"Right. I told you, they paid me to bring your wife."

And here the man added:

"You will drink this drink!"

And with his left hand, he threw me a small bottle of syrup. It's about the size of a finger. He told me with a threatening tone:

"Drink it. Not poison."

"I get it. It contains a powerful anesthetic, right?"

"You have some intelligence now drinks it."

I smiled and said,

"What if I refuse it?"

The man looked at Sarah kneeling under his legs and said,

"You know what's going to happen to her."

"They told you to bring her alive, not dead."

That's when I heard the man's breathing. I probably made him angry with my last phrase.

The man raised his gun in the direction and said,

"They told me to bring it alive, but you have a choice to decide your destiny; either drink it or you die."

Here, I have no choice anymore. This is a man who is not joking. I opened a bottle and then smelled it, and then a man said:

"Drink it, come on."

I took a dose of it. The man became angry, saying,

"Drink it all at once."

I did what I was asked to do. For a few seconds, I didn't feel anything, but I was surprised after that I fell to the ground and everything around me started spinning, and then the darkness covered everything.

I woke up and found myself on the wooden kitchen floor. I got up quickly and found my gun near a table, so I took it and dressed in a sheriff's uniform. Then I called my police colleagues, and police patrols started searching everywhere, and I was with them.

Finally ... It's useless; it's completely gone from the town. And here I remembered something. What did the kidnapper mean?

Is there anyone who hates me in his town? I don't know if we excluded, of course, neighbors. I don't think neighbors kidnap your wife just because they hate you.

Dracul's sect... She is the one who paid him.

Is there a common denominator between the Dracule cult and the kidnapper? Is it possible that a sect asked to kidnap my wife? But why? What is the motive behind that?

I sat in the kitchen with a gun in front of me. Sophia sat next to me, trying to calm me down.

"We'll find her, Jack."

"Sofia... Me- I'm fine. Thank you."

Sofia got up, said goodbye, and sat alone in a house. Where did it disappear? My wife, Sara, what are you doing now?

You see her crying in return for waiting for her unknown fate. I'll find you, Sara. Trust me...

In the Black Swan Pub. I sat on one of the benches, sipping a glass of wine, to calm down my fear for my beloved wife.

It was an empty pub except for Harold, who is my bartender, of course. A big, black-skinned, bald man.

"You heard what happened, Jack. I'm sorry."

I drank a cup inside my hollow.

And here, a crazy idea came to mind.

And I said to Harold:

"Never mind. But I want to know one thing from you. Will you allow me?"

Harold put a towel on his right shoulder like all bartenders do in bars and then said:

"Go ahead."

Here, I told him the following:

"Do you know anything about the Dracule sect?"

I noticed that his pupils dilated for a few seconds and then tried to lie to me, saying:

"No, sir, I know nothing about them."

"Do you have children, Harold?"

"No, sir."

"Good. Now tell me about a sect, and don't try to lie to me."

Sweat began to pour from his black forehead, and he tried more than once to avoid looking into my eyes. Here I used a threatening technique, saying:

"You know lying to the police is a crime punishable by law. Either tell me everything you know about these or... I can take you to the office, and there you will talk."

"I... I can't speak, Jack."

Here I raised my gun in his face, and he stepped back and hit his back against the shelves of cups, and some of them fell and broke on the ground.

He raised his hands in front of his face, saying,

"Please don't kill me."

"This is an option that depends on you!".

"I'll tell you... I'll tell you everything I know. Don't tell me, please!"

You might be surprised by my doing this. But it's a very normal act for me. He refused to tell me, so he forced me to use my threat. Maybe you're wondering about me. Are you a cop? How do you do that?

I'll tell you then. By closing your mouth and getting away from my face.

"Well... Tell me everything you know about them, and no lies, Harold."

"Present.".

I didn't put down my gun, but I held it in front of his face to force him to confess more. He told me:

"They are an evil sect... A sect that controls everything and their being lies in the dreaded moon."

"I want their names right away."

"I don't know much about them, but one day... Scar. That drunken boy, He talked about a cult"

"Scar Tyler?"

"Yes, yes."

"Are you sure that's true?"

"I swear by my wife's life."

"Well... Harold. Are you going to file a complaint against me?"

"No, sir."

"Well. Good expense, please."

"For free, I don't want anything."

Here, I smiled as I got up, but I put on a twenty-dollar bill, and before I went out, I told him:

"Keep the rest."

Scar Taylor lived in a moving trailer on the outskirts of town. And he is a man in his thirties, unmarried. He has black hair and black eyes, and I don't forget the most important note that he has a tattoo on his whole body, as he is one of the characters that love to draw silly tattoos.

Trailer door knocked:

"Scar Taylor? I'm Jack Smith. Sheriff. Open the door."

I got a voice from inside the trailer:

"Who? What do you want?"

Here, I was very angry:

"Open the damn door, or I'll smash it."

Scar Taylor opened the door. So, I went inside quickly, and let me tell you that this is a man who lives in chaos. His clothes are everywhere.

Pictures of naked women fill every spot of his trailer. And let me tell you that I found a blonde-haired prostitute sitting on top of a bed, and I told her:

"Leave immediately."

A prostitute got up and got dressed, and then, before leaving, she said goodbye to Scar, saying:

"Goodbye, darling."

"Goodbye".

Here is what Scar Taylor told me:

"What's the matter, Sheriff?"

But my answer to him was a strong punch with the heel of my gun against his long nose. We'll have fun, rat...

Here is what Scar Taylor told me:

"What's the matter, Sheriff?"

But my answer to him was a strong punch with the heel of my gun against his long nose. So, he fell to the ground on a trailer. Blood was pouring out of his nose as he said,

"Why did you hit me?".

"Shut your mouth."

I immediately put my gun on his head as I told him:

"You have two choices: either you die or you live. Choose?"

The features of terror began to sculpt a white face, which encouraged me to continue in the role of the ruthless criminal.

"Please don't kill me."

Why do they always say this silly sentence, whether in movies or stories? If someone wanted to kill someone else, it would be impossible to give you a chance to even breathe! Maybe in cases of revenge, for example. Maybe you are given some moments to savor lust as revenge, but this is another topic.

I pressed the gun to his head more and said,

"I told you to choose."

"R... Live... I want to live."

Here I told him:

"Get up quickly."

So, Scar got up, holding his nose, which was pouring blood from my strong blow, and I pointed to the bed where a prostitute was sleeping on top of it and said:

"Sit on a bed."

So, Scar sat down and almost swore that his body was trembling like a child. To this degree of death.

I told him, still pointing a gun at him:

"You told me you wanted to live... Fair enough... This is a suitable option. Tell me where my wife is."

"Jack, I'm --.".

"You don't know where it is, right?"

Scar lowered his gaze to the ground and said,

"Yes. I don't know."

"Well. This is your first lie."

And I pulled out the gun to prepare for the killing.

Scar got up from the bed and said,

"I swear a-... Know... I don't know... I -".

"This question determines your life. But sit down first."

Scar sat down again; sweat was wetting his chest and forehead, and he almost swore he almost wet his white pants.

I told him:

"You're a member of the Dracule sect, right?"

Scar said to me:

"No. What are you saying, man? I don't know who you're talking about."

That's where a volcano of anger started to rise. Out of my coat pocket, I took out the muffler nozzle. And I prepared a silencer with a gun.

Scar got up and said,

"Yes. I'm one of them. I'm one of them; don't shoot."

What do you expect you to do to him? No, I wouldn't kill him, if that's your idea. Three faint bullets were fired because of a silencer. Next to Scar on a bed, three bullets pierced the bed cover.

That's when I saw Paul covering Scar's underpants. He on himself...

I pointed the gun at his face and said,

"Your last chance. Talk about everything that belongs to a sect, or I'll empty a bullet magazine in your skull."

"I swear I'll talk, but don't kill me."

And he raised his hands, trying to make it appear not to be dangerous.

"Let's talk fast."

"Dracul's sect... You're trying to save the city from a monster. For this, they need to kill a pregnant woman to extract the baby from her womb for the sake of (the brother of the moon)."

I was disgusted to hear the last words and said:

"What? Do you want me to blow your head off?"

"I swear to you in my mother's grave. It's true, sir."

"Monster? A sect trying to save a town from a monster!"

"Sir, you don't understand the meaning very well. The monster is one of the members of a sect. The monster is controlled by (the brother of the moon). The entity that rules from the moon, and to secure the evil of this monster, they have to kill a pregnant woman every year for this operation."

"Nonsense. I don't believe you, pig."

"I swore to you at my mother's grave. I'm not lying. The Dracule sect worships... One of the gods Eldrich worships is Brother of the Moon, who was detained inside the moon itself."

"Goddess Eldrich?! Who the hell are they?"

Scar swallowed and then said,

"An evil cosmic god. Beings coming from the depths of the dark universe. No human mind can see them or imagine how powerful they are."

"Great, from monsters to the world of babies. Very great. Of course, I will not imprison you because it is not suitable for the insane."

Here, a moment of silence came between us. And somehow, I remembered bodies in a cave, and I said,

"Do you know the secret of corpses in that cave in a black forest? Are they vampires?"

Scar's eyes widened, and then he said cautiously:

"Vampires?! No, they are. They were members of the sect in the past."

"I didn't understand; explain more."

"These have received the blessing of the great (brother of the moon), so they were stoned on both sides of the cave to prepare for the coming of He."

"Who?"

"Brother of the Moon".

That's where I lowered my gun and Scar breathed in happiness, but... I decided not to leave him for a moment, so I raised my gun again in his face, and suddenly I erected with signs of fear still on him:

"You said there was a monster! Fair enough... What kind of monster are you talking about?"

No one knows what he looks like. And as far as I know, everyone who saw a monster never saw light again!

Did you know? He's an idiot. He uses a cheap method, as in some horror stories.

I told him:

"The last question is: Where is my wife?"

"Believe me, I don't know where it is. But often a ritual is held in a cave."

"Vampire cave?"

"Yes. It is there where you will—and swallow his throat—sacrifice your wife to extinguish the raging spirit of the beast."

There was a question knocking on my head, and I said:

"You told me that a sect owns the beast and that the beast is one of them. Fair enough... Why don't they kill a monster?"

"We can't. A monster was a curse from the brother of the moon, and even if you kill the beast, the curse will be transmitted to a member of a sect. Even if all members of a sect die, a curse will be associated with their grandchildren or children."

Here I asked a question:

"Who is the head of the sect? Where does the sect of the beast hide?"

"We don't know each other. Our meetings are held in a cave around fires. And let me show you something so you can believe me."

Here is the most prominent scar tongue out of his mouth. And here I saw a blue sign that looks like a satanic star that you see in cheap horror movies...

"What is this?"

It's damn. Of course, I don't mean ".

"Wait! I don't understand. Are you trying to say that a monster is a human?"

"Exactly... At midnight, you will resist the ritual of sacrificing your wife. And at that moment, you will only have two options."

I raised my eyebrows and said, wondering:

"Two options? Is that a threat, Scar? And I moved my gun to scare him a little.

But Scar responded:

"Either you save a town from a monster but sacrifice your wife and child... Or save your wife, but the consequences will be dire."

"What do you mean by serious consequences?"

"If you save your wife, you will unleash the beast because the seal will weaken at that moment, and then you will free a monster from a pot... And of course, you know what he's going to do with the town."

"The strongest monsters can't face bullets."

Scar wiped the sweat from his forehead, saying,

"You don't understand, sir. I'll tell you something clearer. You currently own the fate of the town in your hands. Either you sacrifice your wife to save a town or you save your wife—assuming you can save her—but you will shoot a monster at a town of cucumbers with your own hands, sir."

I approached Scar and put my gun on his forehead, then lowered my head to a low level, looked into his brown eyes, and said,

"The human race or my wife... I will choose my wife and let the human race go to hell."

Silence.

I turned to get out, but I stood at the door and looked at Scar, saying,

"Two things... Run away from his town immediately. Second, don't try to file any complaint against me, Clear?".

"Clear, sir."

"Good"

At midnight

I parked my car at the entrance to the forest with two police cars in each car. There are two people because the damn town of Norn has only four cops!... Even if you ask for support from

Capital, it's going to take a while. About a week at best, especially with this very cold atmosphere.

I got out of the car carrying a gun. And she smoked a cigarette quickly while Tamari prepared her gun. And Sofia too.

Sophia told me:

"Are you sure of what I said?"

"Yes. Scar told me every detail about a monster. And the bodies of the stranger. And the gods are universal. Etc... And from this nonsense, I knew that there was a sect that intended to sacrifice my wife for the sake of a God who would dwell on the moon!"

Then I said to the team out loud:

"Ready?"

Everyone replied, "Yes, Sheriff Bailiff.".

"Let's go, guys."

As we walked in the snow with our shoes, a shadow emerged from behind trees.

"Stop where you are!" and everyone raised their weapons.

"Woo. Calm down, guys. That's me."

I looked at his black glasses and said,

"Michael, what are you doing here?"

"Nothing just hunted a deer or a rabbit."

And of course, he was carrying a sniper rifle with him. Raising his eyebrows, Michael asked:

"Is there a problem, Commissioner?"

"Nothing. I want you to go home. Clear?"

"Of course. Is there a particular problem?"

Sophia said:

"It's none of your business. Leave immediately."

It's in Sophia's nature that she talks strictly to everyone. And this was so annoying to everyone he met that, as far as I knew, she was the second most hated figure in a town... You might be wondering about the center of the first one, yes, gentlemen, is Mayor Harry.

Michael is out of our way. And of course, the night had come, carrying darkness everywhere, and we could not light flashlights because this is something that exposes us. And so on, after a while. We arrived at a cave, and here we hid behind a giant brawl. In front of us, Sarah was crying as she was tied to a wooden pole, and around her were about twenty people wearing white masks and white cloaks as well.

I don't know why Scar's voice came to mind, saying:

"A sect that is not evil. You're trying to calm the beast by sacrificing your wife."

Thoughts flicked from my head, and Mary approached as she said:

"What are we going to do?"

"Go east and then get distracted, and Sam and I will save Sarah."

"Why don't we just go out to them?" Sam said it with obvious stupidity.

And here I forgot to tell you... Sam, the second man after me. Excuse me; I forgot to introduce you to him.

Sam said:

"Look at them. These are fanatic religious sects. If you go out, you'll only see monsters that want to tear apart."

Sophia said:

"Are we moving forward with a plan now?"

"Come on."

Two girls moved with their guns to the east while Sam and I waited for a suitable moment. But there's Sara's imam. Someone was wearing a cloak. A blue cloak is different from all the white cloaks worn by everyone around him; this is their leader, without a doubt.

But for a few seconds. A person took down an abaya from his body to appear naked, and it turned out that this, or, let's say, this... Girl ... How do you know? She has a long braid. And you rarely find a man with a long braid if he is only from Viking...

And the blue moon appeared in the sky and shined its light on the trees. Earth... The leaves of a tree

Then, for seconds, I saw in front of us a scene, because of which my mind almost stopped.

The girl started kneeling as if she were in pain from something, and suddenly a long tail protruded from above her buttocks, and black hair began to grow all over her body, and her legs turned into goat legs.

And her chest gained clear muscles. As for her head, it turned into a bull's head. With horns and a snout that blows white smoke.

I felt terrified, mixed with fear, and my weapon fell on the ice against my will.

Sam said to me, his eyes almost coming out of their quarries in shock:

"What's that?!"

She replied after I lifted my gun: "Hang on, man."

My wife, Sarah, started screaming as she saw the monster approaching her. While all the sects read like poetic hymns, I think it's a kind of prayer or begging. Or something I don't know anything about.

I looked at Tamari and Sofia and gave a signal.

And the battle began.

The two girls came out from behind trees, screaming:

"Don't move. Police are surrounding a place."

But the beast turned to them and moved to her. From the top of the hill, me and Sam see in front of me a group of men from a sect. Of course, I did not hesitate for a single moment, so I fired a barrage of bullets from my pistol.

A bullet penetrated someone's head and detonated him like a children's balloon.

Another person came with a knife. I thought these were men who didn't carry weapons. But I was wrong...

I shot the man in the stomach. The man rushed back a few meters to fall with his stomach pierced.

Sam also did not hesitate. So, he was shooting left and right.

Sam shouted after blowing someone's head off:

What are you waiting for? Save your wife!

I ran, and I was shooting here and there. To everyone who stands in front of me, no mercy. They are the ones who wanted that. So, they take responsibility.

I went up the podium. And here I saw my wife's face and tears in her eyes.

"Jack".

" Sarah. I came to save you. Don't worry, honey."

And I cut the ropes with the knife I carry. Then she and I ran. I shouted at Sam:

Come on, Sam."

Sam shot one of them, and then we fled a place after we committed a real massacre. These are evil people.

Sam, I, and my wife were running. Sam said to me:

"Sofia and Tamari!."

She replied to him:

"Don't worry, they killed the monster and fled like us."

But we heard Sophia screaming as she said:

"Help me!"

We stopped suddenly and looked back. Sofia was limping, and blood was covering her clothes.

And here we saw radiant red eyes behind Sofia.

For a second, I couldn't believe what he saw.

A monster caught Sofia. By her hair and lifted her in the air as she struggled to let her go.

Then the monster grabbed her by one of her feet. To tear it in half like a piece of paper.

Sam shouted as he fired his gun:

"Sofia... No, no."

I didn't hesitate for a moment. Sarah and I continued our way out of the woods.

Outside, our cars were parked. We rode in a car here. Sam's head hit the glass of our car and then fell into the snow.

I moved the car and then started driving at its speed.

And I look sometimes behind me and sometimes in front of me.

Sarah said in tears:

"I'm scared. We're going to die."

"No, sweetheart. I exist Nothing will happen to you, believe me."

I was expecting the monster to appear at any moment for.

In front of us or behind us. Or even if it's on top of the car.

But we got to his town. And then we entered our house...

I told her:

"Pack all your stuff. We're leaving this town."

I looked through the glass. And here I saw someone running with something in his hand. And for a few seconds, I avoided the window.

Something pierced the window to start burning. Molotov ... I took off my jacket and tried to put out the fire. But gas was faster than me.

Sarah came down screaming, and I told her:

"The back door. Quickly."

She and I ran. Then we opened the door and found in front of us a man carrying a racket.

Of course, he was one of the members of a sect.

It blew his head off with one bullet, and he fell dead.

We ran towards the car. Sons of. They ripped the tires off the four cars. Now what did he do?

Sarah told me:

"What do we do?"

I told her:

"I have a plan."

And in my car, there was a box with four grenades in it. So, I took out two of them and told her:

"Carry this!"

"I've gone crazy."

"Just carry it!"

Sarah picked up two of them, and then we ran through the streets of town. On the way, I found the four from a sect. And they didn't wear masks.

One of them, who had a red beard, said,

"You are destroying a town... The beast will not calm down."

And here the monster jumped on the roof of one of the houses next to us, and we heard a raging bellow sound as it jumped in our direction.

We ran back while she looked behind me.

I found a monster killing two of the sect's men while the other two were trying to kill the monster.

Everywhere around us.

Screams were getting louder. The town's houses started burning suddenly. You see smoke rising from the gray clouds.

While the blue moon had risen high and prominent amid the gray clouds.

We entered one of the houses and then closed the door behind us. Fortunately, it was an empty house. Maybe its inhabitants migrated a few moments ago.

I was in front of the door with my gun raised and my hands shaking. Not out of fear, of course, but from extreme tiredness and fatigue.

And here Sarah said to me:

"What are we going to do? The town is being destroyed!"

Told:

"Don't worry, honey, everything will be fine."

We're third. Me, her, and We know that the sentence that was said above...

Just a white lie: things have always been going against their usual course.

Here, we heard knocks on the door. It's as if someone hit the door with an axe.

She shouted out loud:

"you sons of--."

Of course...

Strong knocks continued on the door, especially after they heard my screams. And here, I heard the sound of glass breaking from behind us.

I turned around, and Sarah stepped back behind me.

I saw a man wearing a mask, holding a cleaver in his right hand, running towards me. I shot him. It hit his right leg. So he fell to the ground and started to groan from pain and the blood that started to cover the floor.

I went forward toward him, and I tightened my grip on my gun.

The man with a mask raised his left hand as he said:

"Mercy".

"No mercy to you."

And a bullet was fired into his head. This is a true mercy.

And all of a sudden, We heard the sound of the door being smashed behind us. Sarah screamed as she stepped back from the door.

So I saw

The axe head is trying to smash the door.

"Go to the second floor."

Sarah went up to the second floor. While I stood waiting for the door to break down,

The man continued to smash the door.

But I stepped through the door. And then, with my left hand, I opened it.

And for a few seconds. A man was raising his axe, intending to strike the door that I opened.

I raised my gun, and a bullet came out faster than an axe.

His head exploded and fell on the steps of the house. Out ...

Fires were starting to take a dangerous turn. The men of the sect were masked, wreaking havoc and destruction here and there.

And the beast is absent; we don't know where it is.

Houses are looted and burned. Cars break the men of a sect kill the townspeople sounds scream everywhere

I closed the door quickly, and I saw three men coming.

This door won't last long.

I threw a pistol. After he finished bullets, I filled a new store. The first man opened the door, and I was greeted by a bullet. So, he fell dead on the ground, but two

Hide beside the door.

Someone said to me:

"Surrender, Jack. The town was destroyed because of you."

Another man said:

"You preferred your wife to a town. What a selfish person you are."

One of them said:

"Look at the blue moon; it's really beautiful!!".

And then I only saw Molotov throwing in my direction.

I backed down in the last seconds.

Molotov fell to the ground, and fire spread everywhere at hellish speed.

Two men ran away.

I tried to go up to the second floor, but the fire was faster than me. She cried out loudly:

Sarah! Sarah! Don't come down."

Sarah's voice came from the top of the floor:

"Jack... Fire!".

"Don't be afraid, dear. Look for a window. About a director Come on."

And I turned to get out from behind the house through the door behind me, overlooking a small garden with a swing and green grass covered with thick white snow.

I looked at the top of the house. I saw a window and shouted:

"Sarah... Sarah."

For a few seconds. Sarah was mostly looking for an exit, and she found the window. But there's a real problem. How are you going to do it?

Sarah opened a window and said,

"How do I get off?!"

My mind was unable to imagine any plan at that moment, so I said to her:

"Jump. Jump out of a window."

"Have you gone crazy? I'm pregnant."

And here I saw nothing but a giant black shadow that fell from the sky on a roof.

My eyes widened as I looked at the beast. A bull's head, a body covered with muscles, a tail that hangs, and a goat's legs, but its height, as I said, is about two and a half meters.

I raised my gun and fired three bullets quickly.

The bullets hit the body of the beast, but they did not affect it, as if they were balls of snow.

What did the monster do at that moment?

It was one of the very hard moments for me. The monster entered from the roof above the house to the inside of the room, and here I saw Sarah being pulled away from a window.

She shouted out loud:

"Sarah... No."

And here, the monster threw something out of my window. He fell at my feet. And when I looked closely...

I only found Sara's upper body.

Here, tears came down, and I went crazy. And she cried:

"Sarah no."

And I knelt on the snow as I hugged Sara's upper body.

And here, the beast threw her underbody at me.

Then he jumped out of a window to land on me.

I heard the sound of his bellows as he approached. And I smelled a bad smell, like a strong sulfur smell, and the black hair that covered his thighs.

She left Sarah's body and looked into his red eyes.

"Son of a... I killed her!"

Snarling a monster and punching me hard, I flew a distance of ten meters.

After it hit the wooden fence that surrounds the house.

I got up on the ice and started to spit blood out of my mouth.

And I'm looking at him. He advances with steps that leave a goat's hoof's mark on the snow.

This is a good moment. I remembered what to keep.

The monster stood on top of my head and then roared as he pressed his leg on my back.

I screamed in pain as I felt a force that was almost tearing my back apart.

And here I rolled over after he lifted his leg from my back.

I looked into his eyes and said,

"Goodbye, son of a--."

Here, his eyes came down red from my eyes to look at what I was holding in my hand.

It was a bomb.

Here, I felt nothing but a white light, and then darkness covered everything.

Done.

Bajaj Spirit

Sajjad stood on the main street waiting for a taxi or a tuk-tuk after the time had passed eleven at night and rain showers were pouring down on their heads ...

"I'm worried about a client, Ali. What? What if we made a mistake?! " Sajjad said with concern evident in his tone.

He replied indifferently:

"Don't worry, I made a clear plan for the agent. All we have to do is find one of the goons and take him to a remote, isolated area."

"But I- "

" Carpets , relax . Notice the amount of benefit that this process brings us. Two carpets alone are sold for three million or more, especially if they are of a new model."

"But we will kill an innocent person!!"

"The end justifies the means, Sajjad."

Sajjad breathed audibly, and Ali noticed Sajjad's nervousness, so he patted his left shoulder calmly, saying:

"Our dream is to get out of Iraq. For this reason, we will kill, steal, and do everything for the sake of our dream. Nothing makes a person crazy or obsessed like a dream."

Then Ali added:

" Relax, Sajjad , I have a sharp knife, and you have one, right?!"

Sajjad felt a knife in the back pocket of his blue pants and said:

" present " .

Green tick passed by them, blowing his horn loudly.

"No, not that!" Ali said to Sajjad .

Passed by and a driver looked at them with clear contempt.

Minutes passed and a yellow tick came quickly. Ali said to Sajjad :

"Old model, we want a new one."

A tuk-tuk driver honked his horn and did not receive a response from Ali and Sajjad , so he passed them faster.

The rain increased, and Sajjad and Ali began to feel the cold swirling around them like a black cloud, until the perfect opportunity came .

"Stop this!" Ali said to Sajjad .

Sajjad signaled to the driver of a red taxi to stop.

I stopped ticking next to the sidewalk ...

Ali noticed that there were flies gathered on the outside curtain of his curtain... And the number of flies exceeded dozens, which raised Ali's astonishment, especially since it was raining. So how could flies gather in this way?!

The two are presented by a driver ...

A strange smell that almost swore it was a corpse smell...

From inside your tick...

The driver had a strangely swollen and swollen face.

A fly hovers over his head, then lands on it, then flies off again...

Were devoid of any sparkle, and his eyes were almost closed from extreme sleepiness and fatigue, as was evident.

He was A young driver in his twenties with a beard and light moustache, and as is clear to Ali and Sajjad...

This driver is a perfect victim...

He is mentally and physically tired because he smells so dirty that flies gather inside his tick just as they collect outside it.

Ali said With a malicious smile :

" Hello ".

The young man responded with a tired nod of his head to Ali. Ali did not care and continued his words:

"We want to go to Al-Khuzam Akhdar. My brother's bike is broken down there. How much do you charge?"

The driver shook his head in agreement to go.

Said while Sajjad was clearly trying to calm his tension: "We will give you 10 thousand, okay?"

The driver shook his head in agreement.

He came up to me thinking within himself - What a fucking idiot - Sajjad sat next to Ali and started ticking towards the green belt.

Ali continued talking to the driver all the way, trying to remove suspicions from them, even though the driver did not speak to me.

Sajjad smokes a cigarette to calm his fear and tension from the operation...

Sajjad looked at the raindrops that were falling next to Taktak and heard the sound of their falling on Taktak's red curtain, and the cold wind had clearly increased in speed.

Ali pulled a pack of cigarettes from his pocket after he stopped talking to the silent driver...

Sajjad thinks about how they will carry out the blind operation and how he will sleep on the money that he will pile up in the form of a bed for him to sleep on like villains in American soap operas...

The tick recorder started working on its own, strangely.

Ali raised his eyebrows and said to the driver:

"How did you turn on the recorder?!" Ali did not see the driver doing anything to turn on the tape recorder.. So how do I turn on the tape recorder??

There was confusion in the voice of the recorder, and the three heard a frightening sound:

"Hello, two thieves !"

Ali felt his stomach tighten when he heard the word " thieves ."

Ali quickly said to the driver:

"Turn off the recorder please , my head hurts ."

The driver did not respond, and Ali and Sajjad heard the sound of laughter from inside a recorder saying:

"I'm talking about you... Ali and Sajjad.."

Adrenaline flowed through their arteries and Sajjad almost screamed when he heard his name inside the tape recorder. As for Ali, his eyes widened in horror as if he heard the news of his death.

"Turn off the damn record." Ali said to the driver again.

The driver did not respond either, so Ali got up from his seat behind the driver and touched the turn off button for the recorder...

An electric current ran through his body at the same moment he touched a button.

He shouted at me, uttering a kind of slumber in a loud voice as he fell back into his seat.

"Are you well?! ." Sajjad said as he touched Ali's hand.

"I know you two want to steal your ticket!"

Ali and Sajjad looked at each other and Sajjad said quickly:

"Where does the sound come from?! Is it..."

The eerie voice inside the recorder said:

"You two whores will die!!"

Ali poked Sajjad on the arm and Sajjad looked at Ali Giving the signal to start the operation..

Ali put his hand in his coat pocket while talking to the driver:

" Do you know who we are?! .."

While Sajjad took out the knife from his pants pocket Slowly ...

The two looked at me and the carpet To each other at the same time, then they pounced screaming at the silent driver ..

Ali put the knife on the driver's neck .

While Sajjad placed the knife on the left side

..

Surprise the two - Ali and Sajjad The driver did not show any reaction... Rather, it was as if nothing had happened.

Laughter came from inside the recorder:

"Two little bitches!"

Ali shouted at the driver:

"Stop your damned ticking!"

But the driver was still driving recklessly.

Ali and Sajjad looked at each other, surprised

.

Ali grabbed the driver's hair angrily and pressed the knife blade to his neck.

And ..

While Ali was pulling the driver's hair... His head was pulled out - Completely - From his body ...

Ali found himself clutching ... The head of the driver... Who was smiling, revealing loose yellow teeth and completely black eyes...?

Sajjad shouted at the same time.

Evil laughter came from inside the tape recorder.

In the next moment... A white light shone in front of Takka and all Ali and Sajjad heard was the loud sound of a truck's horn...

The end.

The Distorted

Jack Woke Up from His Bed Realizing That It Was His 14th Birthday He Sat on His Bed Saying "Happy Birthday to Me... Happy Birthday to Me "He Always Had His Birthdays Alone Sometimes with His Mother but Mostly His Birthdays Were Lonely.

He Finished and Dressed Up Then Came Down for A Breakfast with His Family Your Ordinary Despicable Father Raymond and The Gentle Mother Sofia and The Annoying Little Brother Jimmy.

Jack Sat In Front of His Father And Began Chewing His Piece Of Meat When He Heard His Brother Say

"Give Me The Bread You Monster!"

Jack Looked At Him

"How Could You Talk To Your Big Brother Like That!" His Mother Yelled At Him.

His Father Was Drinking Tea When He Looked At Him And Said To Sofia "You Were Supposed To Give Birth To A Human Not a Monster" He Looked

At His Oldest Son With Contempt Jack Kept Eating And Staring At His Own Plate He Was Used To Such Treatment The Only One That Called Him By His Name Was His Mother The Rest Called Him Names Like Freak And Monster As If He Wanted To Be Like This After He Was Finished With His Plate He Glanced At His Mother Who Was Looking At His Father With Blame But The Father Wasn't Interested.

Jack Went Up to His Room and Washed His Hands and Face He Looked at The Mirror and Stared at His Disfigured Face Completely Burned to the Point Where You Can See the Nerves Jack Suffered Congenital Malformation from When He Was Born to Make Him Look Like This "When Are You Going to Die Monster"

Jack Said To Himself On the Mirror Then He Got Out Of The House Looked Up And Saw That It Was Cloudy

Which Meant Rain Swift Wind And All The Villagers Has Gone To Their Work.

He Walked Holding A Book He Bought From The Nearby City Called The Artistic Way Of Life By Joseph Langdon Jack Was Talented With Art Since Childhood Crossing The Little Door In The Fence

That Surrounded His House Like A Circle He Began Walking To The Forest That Was Undoubtedly The Perfect Place To Draw In.

While He Was Heading Down A Hill He Glanced A Couple Of Young Boys He Knew Planting In a Garden One Of Them Looked At Him And Whispered To The Others Now They All Were Looking At Him And Laughing Like He Was Some Kind Of A Freak He Knew They Were Saying That It's Pretty Obvious By Now But He Didn't Mind Them

He Kept Walking Until He Reached A Vast Field Of Wheat There Were Some Kids Playing Tag Near It As He Watched He Remembered His Childhood And All The Unpleasant Memories With It.

Naturally As A Child None Of The Kids Agreed To Play With Him They Always Threw Clay At Him Whenever They Saw Him

We Don't Want To Play With You Monster! Said One Of The Lot The Others Cheered Him...Broken And Defeated He Went Home Later That Day And Was Surprised By The Slap His Father Gave Him "How Many Times Have I Told You Not To Leave Your Room" He Spat At Him.

But His Mother Intervened And Told Him To Go Upstairs As He Walked The Stairs He Heard Them Arguing "I Didn't Want You To Give Me A Monster!"

A Yell From The Kids Brought Jack Back Apparently He Was Standing Still Thinking When Some Of The Kids Noticed Him And Started Screaming...He Smiled And Resumed His Way To The Forest When He Entered He Saw A Strange Figure In The Distance When He Got Close He Saw That It Was A Man Digging A Hole He Got Closer To Talk To The Man Then He Noticed That It Wasn't Actually A Hole But A Grave.

The Man Was Wearing A Tuxedo Like The Ones Jack Saw Usually When Going To The Nearby City His Hair And Eyes Were Also Black And He Had A Strange Necklace With The Letter S Engraved On It.

"You Came In The Right Time" Said The Man "Um...Who Are You? You're Not One Of The Village Folk"

Smiling The Man Said" Right I'm Not One Of Them But I'm Everything In This World"

Jack Looked Puzzled For A While "For Whom Are You Digging This Grave?" Asked Jack

"For You Of Course" Answered the Man

Jack Smiled And Said Breathlessly "When Am I Going To Die? No No No...Not When But How" Replied The Man.

Jack Looked At The Black Eyes He Was Beginning To Feel Scared By Now So He Looked Down

"You Expect Me To Believe That?!" Said Jack

"I'm Not Asking You To Believe What's Real Boy" Replied The Man

Feeling Annoyed Jack Ignored The Man And Walked Away Feeling The Stares Of The Man Behind Him Who's That Man? Am I Going To Die? Jack Thought To Himself. Then Finally Getting to His Favourite Spot

A Tree Trunk That Was Surrounded By Beautiful Flower Beds With White Yellow And Red Roses And Beyond Them There Was a Lake He Sat At The Tree Trunk Admiring It Then Began Drawing Until The Night Came That Was His Daily Routine Leave The House

Come Here Draw And Go Back Home. He Walked Until He Reached A New Place He Didn't Know What Or How He Got Here He Felt Like He Was Sleep Walking Turns Out That His Legs Have Brought Him To A Place Everyone Is Afraid Of For An Unknown Reason. He Was Standing In Front Of The Well Of Wishes

Jack Stood There Dumbstruck Not Believing How He Got There He Approached the Well Remembering All The Rumors About It Some People Even Claim That It Can Make Wishes Come True. But At A Price

Jack Thought That This Was Stupid A Well Making Wishes Come True As If

But Deep Down He Really Wanted To Know Because Of This Feeling A Feeling Which Is Stronger Than Others. Curiosity

What If Something Came Out Of It What Am I Going To Do Then?

He Thought "Run You Stupid Monster" His Mind Was Telling Him But Curiosity Prevailed. "Why Not Make A Wish What Can Happen The Worst Is You End Up Having The Thing You Crave So Much"

He Felt Obligated To Try Approaching It And See

He Looked Down In The Well.

Complete And Utter Darkness He Flinched For A Second Then He Saw A Pair Of Yellow Eyes Deep In The Bottom That Made Him Scream Falling Flat On His Back Terrified. He Tried To Run But A Voice Came From Deep Within The Well A Soft And Sweet Feminine Voice

"JACKIE, I KNOW WHAT YOU WANT" He Stopped

And Glanced Back Where Did The Voice Come From? Wiping The Dirt Off His White Shirt And Black Pants He Said "Where Are You?"

"COME CLOSER DON'T WORRY I WON'T HURT YOU" The Soft Voice Replied

"No I'm Not That Stupid!"

"DON'T YOU WANT A WISH?" Replied The Voice.

Feeling Skeptical He Said "You'll Make Any Wish Come True?" A Moment Passed And He Didn't Hear Anything

"ONLY ONE" Said The Voice

Smiling He Said "In Exchanged For What? - It Can't Obviously Be For Free " Jack Said To Himself

He Heard The Voice Laughing Menacingly.

"FOOD...YOU'LL BRING IT TO ME"

" What Kind? " Said Jack

"THE SOFT AND JUICY KIND LIKE YOU!"

Jack Felt Terrified And Stepped Back "No...I Can't Do That"

After All Today Was His Birthday And He Wasn't About To Commit A Murder

"THEN THERE'S NO WISH FOR YOU GO" Said The Voice Angrily Jack Picked Up His Book And Ran Home.

When He Got There He Silently Climbed The Stairs But A Female Voice Said "Where Have You Been?" It Was His Mother

He Spun Around And Tried To Look Guilty This Trick Worked Most Of The Times With Her "I Was Drawing Mom" He Said

"You Were Supposed To Come Back Two Hours Ago" Said Sofia Jack Lowered His Eyes Made A

Sad Face And Said "I'm Sorry Mom"

He Felt Her Hands on His Shoulders "Don't Apologies I'm Just Worried About You" She Said Giving Him a Hug "Oh and I'm Sorry I Didn't Be with You on Your Birthday "

Seat heart He Watched Her Then Said Good Night and Gone Up to His Room for A Good Night Sleep but He Couldn't Close His Eyes That Night.

All He Was Thinking Was That Voice In The Well Making Wishes Come True At A Heavy Price...People!

The Next Day He Went To The Forest And Kept Thinking About The Voice When Night Came He Decided To Go Speak With It Again He Stood Near The Well And Said "Hey Do You Hear Me?"

He Glanced At The Bottom The Yellow Eyes Looked At Him He. Stepped Back And Said "I Want To Make A Wish"

"AH I KNEW YOU'LL COME SOONER OR LATER" Replied The Voice Jack Ignored It And Said

"I Want To Be Beautiful"

"FOOD FIRST THEN WE TALK" Jack Went Back To His Village Thinking How On Earth Is He Going

To Bring Someone To The Well He Exhausted Himself Thinking Then He Went To Bed.

The Next Day Jack Was Walking In The Village And Thinking Of Who Would Be A Good Victim For This He Said Hi To Someone He Knew The Person Waved Back Then It Suddenly Hit Him The

Perfect Victim Ronald Clinton. He Was An Alright Boy With Good Taste In Clothing And His Handsome Face He Was 6 Years Older Than Jack Which Made Him 20 Ronald Was Good Because He Was Different He Didn't Mind Jack But At The Same Time He Didn't Have a Strong Relationship With Him Either.

Jack Stopped And Started A Conversation About The Weather And So On He Needed A Way To Start A Conversation Some How Then Remembering Sarah Coldwin Ronald Was Very Close With Her So He Thought Of A Good Plan Then Said "Ronald I Wanted To Tell You Something".

Ronald Seemed Skeptical Then He Said" What Is It?"

"Sarah Has a Message for You" At These Words Ronald's Eyes Widen and Said "What? How Could She Be Talking With You!?"

Of Course Ronald Was In Love With Her But Jack Didn't Know Any Of This Stuff So He Took This Chance And Said "You Know How Her Family Are Strict About Everything So She Gave Me A Message For You".

Ronald Looked Around to See If Anyone Nearby Is Listening Then Said "What Did She Tell You?"

Jack Smiled And Said "She Told Me She'll Be Waiting For You In The Forest Near The Well Of Wishes" Ronald Stood There Thinking

"Are You Sure?" He Said Jack

Looked At His Blue Eyes And Said "Yes She Told Me That She'll Be Waiting For You In Midnight"

Ronald Thanked Him And Went Home To Prepare For His Last Date While Jack Went To The Forest And Waited Until Midnight He Occupied Himself With Drawing A Strange Tree That Looked Like A Sad Man Crying

When He Finished It Was Close To Midnight So He Went To The Well And Hid Behind A Tree And Started Waiting.

An Hour Passed Then He Heard Foot Steps It Must Be Him Thought Jack A Few Seconds Later There He Was Ronald Saying in a Low Voice "Sarah Where Are You Sarah" He Became Near the Well Now He Heard a Soft and Sweet Feminine Sound Calling Him.

"OH ROOOONAAAALD" He Spun Around

"Sarah Is That You? Where Are You!? "

" I'M IN THE WELL RONALD HELP I CAN'T SEE IT'S REALLY DARK AND SCARY"

He Approached the Hole of The Well and Looked at It "Don't Worry I'll Get You Our-A 20-Foot-Tall Tentacle Like Thing Sprung Out From The Well It Wrapped Itself Around Ronald's Nick And Dragged Him In The Well Hearing The Screaming Jack Pissed Himself And Ran Home As Fast As He Can Saying To Himself

"It's Not My Fault He Got Dragged In The Well".

He Returned Home That Night Saw His Mother On The Fence Waiting For Him

"Mom....Mom There's A Monster In The Forest I Saw It In The Well It Took "

He Stopped What If The Police Turned Up And Came Here Asking About Ronald

"Honey? What Did You Just Say?"

"Um Nothing I Must've Been Dreaming Anyway Good Night"

And He Climbed The Stairs Up And Locked His Room "Don't You Want Dinner?" Said Sofia

"No" He Replied Behind The Door I Can't Tell Anyone They Might Think I Killed Him

But Did I? NO Said Voice In Him He Changed And Got On His Bed And Closed His Eyes Muttering "I Didn't Kill Him I Didn't Kill Him"

Jack Woke Up The Next Day Feeling Refreshed He Got Up And Walked To The Sink He Washed His Hands And Washed His Face He Stopped There Was A Strange Soft Feeling He Looked Up And Saw His Face He Gasped His Disfigured Face With All The Veins Sticking Out Of It Was Normal And Clean With Smooth Skin He

Washed It A Couple Of Times And Hit Himself To Make Sure It's Real.

He Went Down the Stairs Screaming "Mom"

His Mother Was Preparing For Breakfast And Was Holding The Glasses When She Saw Him The Glasses Fell And She Began To Scream Too Later On In The Doctor's Clinic Dr.Bolt Which He Was The Only Doctor In The Village Examined Jack.

The Doctor Smiled And Said This Is Undoubtedly A Miracle Jack Smiled Back I'm Sorry Ronald He Said To Himself They Went Back Home His Father Was Back From His Blacksmith Job He Saw Jack And Told His Wife "Sofia...Who's That With You? "

Jack Felt The Rush Of Hot Blood Rushing In Him "It's Our Son Raymond It's Jack!" Said His Mother.

"Impossible...How Could He Be Jack!?"

Losing Himself Jack Ran Away Upstairs To His Room

And Shut The Door Closed And Slept For Two Hours Then Waking Up He Decided To Go On A Stroll In The Village.

While Walking In The Village Everybody Was Staring At Him Afraid To Even Come Close To Him

He Stared At Them All "Isn't This What You Wanted People!" Said To Himself Then He Decided To Go To The Forest On His Way He Saw The Gang Of Children Who Screamed At The Site Of Him Last Time.

They Didn't Scream This Time But Their Faces Looked Lived With Fear They Scrambled And Then There Were None He Paused "At Least They Just Ran Away This Time" He Said

Maybe They'll Get Used To Me If I Kept At This Routine Every Now And Then Yeah I Think They Will He Told Himself.

But As He Was Beginning To Feel Better He Heard Something That Made His Heart Sank A Police Car! Where Is It? He Followed The Sound And To His Horror The Car Was Parked At The Clinton's House No Doubt Investigating Donald's Disappearance.

It's Fine They'll Never Figure Out Where He Is or What Happened Jack Thought Then He Returned to The Path of The Forest and Spend His Time Drawing as Usual When He Finished It Was

Close To 9 So He Went Back Home but Was Surprised by The Same Police

Car He Saw Hours Ago The Police Are At His Doorstep "Stay Calm They Can't Find Out What Happened" He Told Himself Again

Then Paused To Prepare Himself When He Opened The Door And Saw His Mother And Father Sitting On A Blue Sofa.

And Sitting Opposite Them Was a Thin Man with A Thick Mustache Jack Recognized Him from His Uniform as The Police but Next to Him Sat the Chief a Bald Man Wearing a Monk Robe.

His Heart Sank Deeper "Jack Dear Come Here The Officer Want To Ask You A Few Questions"

Said His Mother He Felt Nervous But He Smiled And Said "Alright"

He Sat Between His Mother And Father. "Jack...How Are You Son?"

Asked The Chief "Fine Sir" Answered Jack Politely but Then the Officer Joined and Spoke

"I'm Officer Clark...I'm Guessing You Heard About The Case Of Ronald Clinton's Disappearance Correct?

Jack Nodded "It's Really Sad"

The Officer Looked At His Eyes.

"You Were the Last Person to See Him Before He Disappeared Do You Know Where He Went or What Happened to Him? "

"No Officer" Replied Jack

"A Few Witnesses Saw You Speaking With Him...What Were You Talking About?"

"Nothing Really We Just Talked About The Weather"

Well At First Anyway He Said To Himself.

"Answer The Question" Said The Officer Still Looking At His Eyes.

Jack Felt A Little Scared But He Improvised And Said "I Was Talking To Him About The Painting He Wanted Me To Draw".

"A Painting? He Asked You To Draw A Painting?"

"Yes" Answered Jack Back

"Why Does He Wants A Painting? And To Whom? Did He Tell You The Reason? "

" No Sir" Answered Jack The Officer Paused To Drink Water Then He Said

"Your Mother Told Me That You Were Coming Home Late At Night And It Happened That The Same Time Ronald Went Missing You Weren't In The House So Where Were You? "

Jack's Stomach Gave a Huge Lurch.

How On Earth Did He Forget About This He Has No Alibi! But It Turns Out He Was Right At least About Not Telling Anyone.

"I Was Drawing And I Lost Track Of Time" He Said In A Hoarse Voice The Officer Smiled And Jack Knew He Fell In The Trap

"Your Face Was Disfigured And I Don't Mean Anything By It But All The Town's Folk Including Your Family Told Me That You've Changed In That Aspect So What's Your Explanation For This?".

Jack Felt Pressured And Said "I Don't Know Officer

Maybe It's a Miracle"

"You Believe In Miracles Jack?"

"Yes Sir"

At That Officer Clark Got Up with The Chief They Exchanged Handshakes with The Father but Before They Got Out the Chief Turned and Asked Him

"Jack...Tell Me Where Do You Draw? "

"In The Forest...Why?"

Replied Jack Then He Realized the Grave Mistake He Did

In The Night Jack Sat at His Bed Thinking He Glanced a Blue Light Flashing from His Window Signaling the Rain and Lightning He Looked from The Window Rain Pouring Down at It Little Drops of Water Hitting the Glass He Looked Down His Room Was on The Opposite Side of a Wheat Field

The Field Was Extended As Far As The Eye Can See There Was a Tree In The Beginning Of The Field Jack Stared At It The Blue Light Of The Lightning Flashes Every Now And Then Until He Saw It.

A Black Figure He Waited Until The Next Flash Of Light To See It Clearly It Was An Officer His Bottom Dropped "They're On to Me Now Damn It All" He Returned To His Bed More Paranoid Than

When He Left It Then Finally After What Seemed Like An Hour He Fell Asleep.

In The Morning He Woke Up Washed His Face and Looked at The Mirror His Eyes Widened with Fear He Looked Closer. His Forehead Have Gone Back to Its Ugly Disfigured State

Impossible But Everything Else Seems To Still Be Normal And Soft And Then It Hit Him He Was Turning Back.

He Lowered His Hair So That No One Can See It He Got Down Ate Some Breakfast With His Mother His Father Has Already Gone To Work So He Finished His Breakfast In peace. After That He Went To The Usual Routine He Got Out Of The House But Just Then He Noticed That Someone Was Following Him Everywhere He Go Jack Was Holding His Art Book So He Went To The Forest Naturally The Officer Followed Him.

Jack Sat On A Tree Trunk And Tried To Draw Something But His Mind Kept Lingering On The Officer So He Tried To Make A Plan On How To Speak With The Monster But He Didn't Find Any

So, He Decided to Go Home with No Paintings Except A Few Lines and Circles.

It Went on Like This for A Week Jack Was Being Watched by The Informer He Tried to Shake Him Off but All His Attempts Failed but In the Next Week Jack Was Surprised to See That the Informer Was Gone

Jack Didn't Know If He Was Really Gone This Time Or If He's Just Stepping Up His Game Of Hide And Seek Nevertheless He Seems To Be Really Gone Now.

Jack Took The Chance And Went To See The Monster

As He Stood Near The Well The Sun Was Gone Jack Looked Down The Well And Said

"Hey!?" The Yellow Eyes Appeared

"JACKIE I KNOW WHAT YOU WANT" Said The Voice

"Why Am I Turning Back!?" Said Jack

"BECAUSE YOU DIDN'T BRING ME FOOD!"

"What!? I Brought You Ronald!".

"AND THAT'S NOT ENOUGH JACKIE I NEED MORE"

Jack Clenched His Fist "What Do You Mean?"

"AS LONG AS YOU KEEP BRINGING ME FOOD YOU'LL KEEP YOUR BEAUTIFUL FACE FOR LONGER"

Feeling Angry He Yelled "You Tricked Me!".

"THAT WAS THE PAYMENT FROM THE BEGINNING JACKIE...YOU WANT YOUR BEAUTIFUL FACE BRING ME MORE FOOD"

Jack Yelled "Damn You Monster!"

He Left The Well And The Forest And Gone Back To His House He Sat On His Bed Began Hitting It Until He Passed Out.

In The Next Day He Went Looking In The Village For His Victim Again When He Saw Him

Albert Floyd A Bit Muscular and Tall But That Wasn't The Dangerous Thing About Him Rumors Say That He Loves Children A Little Too Much Jack Was Going To See If They're True.

He Approached Albert Saying" Hi "Albert Stared At Him Jack Was Wearing A Hat So He Could Cover His Forehead But Other Than That The Only Thing Albert Saw Was a Very Beautiful Boy So He Said

"Hi yourself" Jack Smiled Menacingly

"I See That You're A Strong And Capable Of Protecting Someone Small Like Me" Said Jack

"I Can Definitely Help You" Said Albert A Grin On His Wide Face. Jack Took This As A Yes And Kept Going

"I Need You to Meet Me at The Wheat Field Near the Forest That's Where All the Bad Guys Always Chase Me Off So I Can't Go Make a Wish in The Well"

Jack Screwed His Eyes As If He Was Crying Albert Put His Hand On Jack's Head And Started Rubbing Him "When You Need To Go Just Tell Me OK?"

" We Need To Go In Midnight " Said Jack.

Then He Left Albert Thinking He Was Too Nice For His Own Good But Jack Didn't Know What Was Hidden Was Greater.

Jack Got Out Of The House Feeling Positive That Night

He Walked To The Wheat Field Where He's Supposed To Meet With Albert A Kind And Gentleman Figure In Jack's Pure Mind Not Knowing Albert's True Intentions

"I Don't Believe It You Really Came" Said Jack Breathlessly

"Of Course I Wasn't Going To Leave This Bad Guys Hurt A Fragile Poor Thing Like You" Said Albert His Grin Bigger Than Ever

They Walked Until Jack Saw The Well " There It Is! C'mon" He Said.

They Got Close And The Tentacle Sprung Out From The Well It Wrapped Itself Around Albert's Waist With Such Force He Split Him In Two Then Dragged His Body To The Well.

Jack Got Close To See What's Happening Inside But What He Saw Made Him Starts Screaming Like He Never Screamed In His Life.

The End...

Something from the Depths

One of the strangest things that happened today was the presence of that strange corpse that was washed away by the waves of the beach towards our village, the village of Hamilton.

But before I tell you the secret of this stranger's corpse, I bet you won't sleep at night because of it.

We have to go back two days before those strange events.

Two days ago.

I went out to fish as usual at three o'clock in the morning. The sky was still night, and heavy rain was falling over my head like stones.

The inhabitants of the village slept quietly and peacefully.

I carried my things, represented by hooks, and some delicious worms. As for the fish.

Then I left for the shore and got on my boat, which could barely accommodate two people, and I started rowing towards a certain spot.

However, ...

I was surprised by something that surprised me.

Although the night sky...

Except something is glowing under the seawater.

Something blue in color. And it was glowing phosphorus.

I approached a place and realized at that time that this was a blue light.

Making a dark spot different from the water of the lake.

I had an idea that you might find crazy or a bit strange, but I decided to throw the hook and fish over a strange blue spot.

Maybe you're wondering if you've seen this spot before or not.

In fact, no. Yesterday I was in the same place, and there was no blue skylight.

And to confess something to you.

And he... Something attracted me to that spot or that blue light.

It's weird, but it's comfortable. Scary, but reassuring. Strange but beautiful at the same time.

Anyway, I was stationed in the middle of the blue spot, and then I started throwing a hook like I told you and took one of my grandmother's favorite songs as usual, "the sea is our own." this is the title of the song.

Then a fishing rod moved.

So, I knew there was a fish, and I started to pull the pulley quietly.

Then pull a little. The waves move a vehicle a little. It's okay; I'm understanding the sea at this point. Pull quietly. And then I lifted the fish.

However, ...

I raised my eyebrows in excessive astonishment and horror.

When I saw a fish, it had a small human head.

I let out a cry of terror and threw a fish toward the sea with an involuntary movement.

A boat was moved a little by the calm waves.

I took a deep breath and then calmed down. What did you just see?!... It's impossible... A fish with a human head.

I wiped the sweat that came down because of my fear and terror at the sight of a fish's face.

Then I looked towards the sky, and then I looked towards the harbor of a village. Then I pinched myself. Maybe I'm in a dream?...

However, ...

I'm not in a dream. This is the cold atmosphere, heavy rain, calm winds, and the night sky.

The terrifying calm. And the sound of waves crashing into the boat and pushing it right and left. It's all true.

I decided to re-catch a fish for two reasons: first, it is my livelihood. If I do not sell fish, I will die of hunger.

Second, I am the only one who sells fish in our village. If I do not bring fish to the village, I will receive a crowd of insults.

I threw the hook again in the blue spot and started humming my grandmother's song. The sea is ours.

Move the string like a fishing rod.

It's nice! There's prey. I started pulling a fishing rod quietly.

And so on, bit by bit. The fish came out.

Let out a scream of terror again.

A fish fell on the wooden floor of the boat. It was a human head!

A boat is moved by calm waves.

I looked with focused eyes at a human head. His eyes were white as snow, and blood was coming down from both eyes. His nose was cut off, and there was nothing in his place but a black hole.

He doesn't have eyebrows or eyelashes. His skin is like dead skin, pale and white, devoid of any soul.

The strange thing is that there is a fish or an object that he caught that did not move and did not try to jump back into the water.

As if he doesn't want to go back to the water.

Lucky for me, I have a small stick, which I use to kill fish sometimes, so I took a stick and started moving the strange fish.

No movement.

Strangely, I have never seen anything like this in my life—a fish with a human head—this is something you only see in nightmares.

What should I do now?...

The dawn boat is at an end, and tomorrow morning, dozens of idiots will stand up to buy fish from me.

I decided to take this fish to show it to the people of the village and especially to our leader.

Carter salmon is a leader, and he'll know what to say when I show him this scary creature.

In the following hours...

Guess what you hunted?

Twenty fish with a human head...

I put the exotic fish in a big bag, and then I started rowing towards the port.

I tied my boat, and then he carried a bag behind my back, and I set off towards the village leader, carter.

He has to see this; no one can buy a fish with a human head to eat it.

Unless it's Vander. And if you don't know, then he's...

He holds the title of the craziest person in a village.

I reached the cabin of carter's leader in the center of the village and quietly knocked on the door, I heard a voice from behind the door saying:

Who is it?

" I'm peter, sir, a fisherman."

I opened the door, and carter appeared, with his bald head, gray mustache, and belly that extended for about two meters! Carter, playing with his moustache, said,

" What has brought you now, peter?"

" Sir, I have to see this..."

You're probably wondering what carter said about the exotic fish you caught. Here's what he said:

" it's just fish, peter! "

He grabbed the fish that was placed on a table in front of carter and lifted it in front of his face, saying,

" it's not an ordinary fish; look, it has a human head."

Carter laughed and played with his gray mustaches, saying:

" We have one Vander, and that's enough for the village. I don't want--"

I interrupted him as I squeezed my teeth.

" I'm not crazy, carter. Look in front of your eyes; don't you see it?"

" Peter, do you have a disease?"

" I'm not sick; I'm telling you the truth: it's not a natural fish."

" But I see them as natural fish! "

I raised my eyebrows from excessive shock, then put a fish back in a bag and went out of carter's house angrily towards my house.

This is what happened between us, but the strangest thing you have not heard yet

I opened my store and put fish in their place.

I'm sure all will come and see these ugly fish, and no one will buy them.

It's okay. I have some money to help me survive for several days.

" Nice fish, peter!"

This was Casper, our village blacksmith, always buying fish from me early in the morning.

I said to Casper:

" Are you out of your mind?"

Casper raised his eyes and raised his eyebrows in surprise, saying:

" Excuse me."

" These are fish; they have a human head."

" Casper looked at the fish and then looked into my eyes, saying,

Are you drunk again? You drink a lot of alcohol!"

" I'm not drunk; look at it, it's a hideous fish!"

Casper took a fish, smelled it, looked at it with concentration, and then said to me:

" it's a normal fish; are you okay, peter?"

" I'm not well! "

I yelled at Casper, and Casper took two steps back, saying:

" Why are you so angry?! Peter, I'm... I didn't."

" I don't sell fish; go from here, come on, go."

Casper left a fish, and then I left away while he was staring at me with skeptical looks. Damn him.

Within the following moments, I quarreled with five other fools, like Casper, screaming at the top of my voice:

They are fish with a human head; do you see them, fools?

One of them laughed.

" These are good jokes, peter, but I am hungry and not in the mood for them."

" you idiot, I don't make jokes. Look at it. Come on."

And I raised one of the fish in their face. Everyone looked at me with their eyes in the height of astonishment, but I was the one who was at the top of astonishment.

How can they not see these terrifying fish?! Have they lost their minds?!

I entered into a heated discussion between me and these idiots that ended with the expulsion of those from my store, and then I closed the store and did not sell a single fish to them.

In the afternoon, carter came to me with two fools, one of whom is will the blond, and the other is carter's little brother Simon, who is unlike his older brother.

His body was as thin as a match.

Sitting on a chair in front of my kitchen table, carter said:

" Peter, I've got some – "

" You don't need to explain; I'm not going to sell a single fish to them; it's a cursed fish."

Will blonde and Simon looked at each other in astonishment, and then carter spoke again:

" Peter, there is nothing strange about these fish that you catch; they are very natural fish!"

" Natural?! Oh my god, have we all become crazy or blind?! Look at this fish well—and peter picked up one of the fish on his table—look well, it has a human head, do you see?! These are white eyes, and this is a severed nose! Look well..."

Will blonde laugh with Simon with a loud laugh, and carter ignored the sound of laughter behind him and told me:

" Peter? Are you okay? Two days ago, you were acting strange!"

Simon, carter's little brother, said:

" Peter, your father was a village madman, so don't be like him."

Here I threw a terrifying fish in Simon's face, Simon was disgusted when the fish hit his face, and he shouted angrily as he curled his fist:

" Why did you do that?!"

" Get out, get out of my hut."

" How dare you kick us out of your house?"

Squeeze will blond his fist is another, and horror and fear mixed with anger seemed to settle inside my body, and squeeze my fist was ready to fight had it not been for carter's rise, who raised his voice loudly:

" All of you stop."

Simon shouted at his brother:

" He threw a-- "

" I said, stop, woe take Simon outside."

" Carter!"

" Simon, we'll talk in a little bit. Come on, go outside."

Simon and will stared at me with angry looks, wanting quick revenge, and calmed my nerves a little. Carter said while still standing in front of me:

" Peter, you didn't have to do this to my brother."

" He started it. He has to bear the consequences."

Carter sighed and played with his gray mustaches.

" Peter, look, you know me; I like to hear from all sides. These are fish on a table that has nothing; they are ordinary fish, peter."

" But I see it as something else."

" Maybe because of alcohol, don't forget to always get drunk, peter."

" I'm not drunk now, carter."

" I know this, but you say something hard to believe: that these are fish that have the right human head?"

" Correct."

" Good, I have to tell you something, but first sit on a chair."

I sat on a chair while carter sat beside him and looked into my eyes concentrating, then spoke in a strange whisper:

" Peter, I know that something lurks in this village—something evil and inhuman. I'm sure of it."

I raised my eyebrows, saying:

" I didn't understand "

" Yesterday, I saw something strange coming out of a blue spot that is near the port, something strange, but I don't know how to describe it to you.

It was total darkness, and I was standing on the harbor to see the skyline.

You know, it's my favorite habit, and there I saw... I saw him come out."

" What did you see? "

Something that looked like an octopus, but it was half-upper... Girl: yes, a had red hair, and his lower half was an octopus.

And its length...

You won't believe me. But his height was two meters.

What did I do?

I don't remember, except that I decided to run away and not tell this story. Maybe it was just a hallucination because of the darkness and the waves of the sea.

Maybe you're delusional. Don't forget that rocks in darkness appear differently.

I mean, you are under the illusion that you see something, but it turns out that it is just a stone or a rock.

Why are you telling this story, carter?

I tell it so that you believe me. On the same side, I feel that there is something very evil surrounding this village; maybe there is a mysterious secret or a curse I don't know, but at the moment, you have to sell fish to everyone, even if it is with a human head.

-however--...

Carter interrupted me as he played with his mustache again; this was his second favorite habit.

" don't tell me "But." at night, meet me outside our village. We will go to a hill, to Vader's house. You know that he is a magician and a great sorcerer. We will take one fish for you to show him."

Carter interrupted, saying:

" But he's crazy, sir -- "

" I think he knows more than us, so we call him crazy. Anyway, we will go to him at night; do not forget at night."

Carter came out, and I remained amazed by this conversation that took place between us, but despite that, I was very relaxed. Some believe me...

Finally...

At night, I brought a fire lantern with me as I met carter, he was holding a gun behind his shoulder, and he quickly said to him:

" In anticipation of... Precaution "

And he walked together towards a hill that rises above our village, where Vander's hut was located—a quiet, silent, and at the same time fishy hut.

But as soon as we got home, we saw... The strangest thing we have seen in our lives...

When we arrived at the hut, we found Vander, naked of any clothes, kneeling in front of a wooden statue in the form of a man with a snake's head, ibex horns, bat wings, etc. Vander was saying, not knowing we were behind him:

Oh great, bless me. Forseken, the maker of destinies, and its destruction. The one of kind is the creator of existence, the destroyer and tamarth, the god of death and the dead, the cosmic lizard, the mother of darkness, the great serpent, devoured by the planets, the white shadow, and the messenger of cosmic entities. (Incomprehensible words) belgaoth is the creator of the stars. Dinner. The sleeper in eternal slumber. (Incomprehensible language) psiphon, the master of superhuman beings. Samael the creator of the light of the sun and the light of the great (incomprehensible language) ... (incomprehensible language)

" Vander... "

Carter spoke as he grabbed his gun. Vander turned around and gave us two spiteful looks as if we had interrupted his prayers, and he got up quickly and shouted at us loudly:

" What do you want from me?! "

Carter spoke calmly:

" Vander, calm down, please. Did you worship this wooden statue? ..:"

Vander's eyes widened, and he looked at a statue and said:

" it's none of your business; what do you want?"

" We want to ask you some of our questions."

" Nope, just go from here; I won't answer any questions."

Carter laughed:

" of course, you will answer my questions."

Vander raised his right eyebrow in wonder and said,

" What are you going to do? Are you going to shoot me with your gun?"

Carter looked at his gun and then looked at Vander and said,

" No, but I will tell you, the people of a village, that you worship wooden statues, and you know that the people of the village are very fanatical about their religion. Do you remember the last time I saved you from their hands when they found books of black magic in you?"

That was an incident three months ago, where some complaining boys sneaked into Vander's house secretly and stole some books of black magic—about which they knew nothing—and had it not been for carter's intervention that night, the residents of Vander village would have been killed and burned his body on charges of heresy and witchcraft.

Recalling an incident, Vander said:

" Well, it's my freedom; I don't worship."

" Vander, you live among a fanatical and ultra-religious population, and when I tell them that you worship a wooden statue and refuse to help me."

" Well, well, I understood a threat. What do you want from me?"

Carter told Vander:

" we'll talk inside."

And the three of us went inside Vander's dreary and dark hut. I put a fire lantern on an old table next to a collection of old and suspicious books. And what caught my attention the most was that book.

"White book" and under the written author of" halker dwin"... And it was a book with strange leather that did not look like ordinary skin and as if it were made from human skin.

Vander wore a white shirt and torn black pants that were very dirty, and carter said quickly, scrutinizing the hut:

" We want to show you something."

I took a fish out of a bag and then put it in front of Vander's widening eyes. Vander said:

" What is this? "

" Can you see it? "

I told Vander, and Vander answered me:

" of course, it's a fish with a human head."

I looked at carter triumphantly. Carter said quietly:

" Well, what is the secret of these fish? Peter says that all the fish he caught yesterday were human heads."

" I don't know... The what! You thought I knew all the answers to your questions."

" But you're a wizard."

" And what does this mean? ... Let me tell you something, carter... I'm not a magician or a wizard. I am a seeker of superhuman creatures. Great."

" What is the secret of these books?! It's about black magic, Vander."

" of course, I try to build a channel of communication between me and the great ones to get forbidden knowledge."

Vander laughed, and carter and I exchanged skeptical glances, and i said to Vander:

" I didn't understand. Who are the greats you are trying to reach?"

" You are just an ignorant person who does not know what I am talking about. Great.

They are the gods we worship. Immortal and with power that far exceeds your imagination they are masters, and we are slaves."

" Forget this nonsense; tell us the secret of this fish."

" I don't know."

Carter stepped forward to Vander, saying:

" Vander, you know how much I hate lying..."

" And will you believe me when I tell you the truth?! ..."

" Say what you have."

" you'll consider me crazy..."

" You already are, and now tell us what you know so that we can go home quickly."

It was clear that carter was very nervous, and I agree with him on this matter.

The hut is narrow enough to fit two people, not a third, and despite the presence of a fire lantern... Which is supposed to light up a whole hut because it is small in size.

But darkness surrounded everything. And I can say I could barely see Vander and carter in front of me because of the total darkness.

And worse than darkness. It smells like a hut that looks like a lot.

The smell of mold or decaying corpses and spider houses was scattered in every corner, and dust covered almost everything. Until I realized that no one could live in this cottage, even for one day! How does Vander live here?

Carter said quietly:

"Tell us everything you know, Vander... And I'm warning you. Don't lie about that."

" I don't need to threaten you. I'll tell you everything I know. Don't cut me there. There's a pyramid of creatures. This is a pyramid that shows the superiority of each other's beings. There, at the top of the pyramid. The gods are universal, and these are the masters of existence because they existed before him. Like forsaken and the one of kind."

" Complete quickly."

" don't interrupt me... It comes after the cosmic gods, the great, and these are the demigods who have been worshiped by humans and non-humans in the past and until now, and the pyramid descends and descends to other levels... There are five levels of power in addition to the level of the great—the sixth—and the level of the universal gods, which is considered the seventh and final level."

I quickly said to Vander:

" Let me guess: humans are at the bottom of the pyramid."

" Humans are off the list."

Carter said:

" I didn't understand. Explain more"

" Simply ordered... All entities worship entities that are higher than them by force and status. For example, the great ones worship the gods of the universe. And" big things" worship the greats. A great war happened. After the great disobedience, the gods became universal and rebelled against them. But the greats were locked up inside planets on orders from forsaken. After the great lost the battle against the god's cosmic"

" Well."

" I mean that the blue spot that is on the beach is nothing but... Maybe he was imprisoned by one of the greats."

Carter looked at me, and I looked at Vander, and then I said in disbelief:

" Do you mean there is a fictional monster living under a beach near our village? "

" I think so."

Carter laughed and told Vander:

" it's true? Are you crazy?"

" I told you... You won't believe me from what I finished about these things."

" Let me ask you. Where did you get this information from? This book"

Vander pointed to the side of a book next to an oil lantern, the white book and Vander added:

" The author of halker edwin was the first human to communicate with the greats, and he wrote this book in a secret language that i am trying to decipher."

Carter said quietly to me:

" Come on, let's go. It's getting late."

Before we went out, Vander told us:

" This is a village that has become cursed; no one will ever survive it. I advise you to escape from this village immediately."

Carter said:

" And we advise you to stop reading silly horror stories and worship a god other than this ugly wooden statue."

And when I came home, I slept exhausted from all these newest events, but I got pregnant with a strange dream, and with that dream, I saw something scarier in my life...

I dreamed of walking in the middle of a forest the likes of which i had never seen in my life. Trees of different bright colors. Trees with red leaves. Trees with blue leaves. Trees with purple leaves. All colors of the group

However, where am I?

If you are in a dream... Isn't it supposed that I don't feel like I'm in a dream?

I started to look at the beauty of the trees while I was walking. To where? I don't know exactly. But a vague feeling forces me to walk toward something.

And then I reached one of the trees with snowy leaves. A man was digging a hole in a tree trunk.

"Hello," I said in a quiet voice.

A man erected it without turning around for me. He was a man who looked weird. As if he is from a past era. Because his clothes are strange, he wears a long coat with a split tail and flutters with the calm winds. A man said in a very deep voice:

"Monsters are everywhere; you will become one of them, sooner or later.".

And the man turned around slowly. And I saw...

I saw his eyes. He had sharp eyesight, and he was wearing a purple vest under a coat, a white shirt under it, and resting on a crutch. I noticed that he was wearing two rings, one silver on the middle finger and the other gold on the little one's finger.

"Who are you?" I said to the man, strange.

"Forsaken".

"Forsaken? I've heard that name before!".

"of course, I am the master of the gods, cosmic! But now look at a grave, peter."

"How do you know my name?! ".

A man named forsaken laughed sarcastically and said,

"I know what exists and does not exist!"

"I didn't understand?!"

"You don't need to understand; look at your grave."

I raised my eyebrows, asking:

"My grave! Am I going to die? How? Why? ".

The darkness covered the world around us, and I thought that a dream had disappeared, but I was surprised to find forsaken saying to heaven:

"The great serpent, my favorite animal!".

And I looked at the sky at that time... And I wish I hadn't seen the sky of...

He has yellow eyes. One of them, I almost swear, is the size of a planet! A big snake. It was so big that it covered the ground and lit

I screamed and woke up from a nightmare. I looked at my clothes. It was very wet from sweat. I got up from the bed and walked towards the kitchen to drink water.

Early in the morning...

I heard a loud knock on the door. I was tired, so i hadn't slept since i saw the terrifying nightmare.

"Carter!".

As he contemplated my situation, carter said:

"Your eyes are red?! Have you slept well? Anyway, you have to see this!".

I dressed and then went out with carter towards one of the houses that is located in the south of the village. All the residents were gathered at a house in a disturbing scene.

I told carter:

"what's up? What happened?".

"You will see; come on, come."

Carter spread some men out at the door, and we entered a house. There was a little girl, no more than ten years old, who was sitting on the back of a wall at the entrance to the room with the harshest signs of terror on her face. Her eyes were wide. She was holding the girl's hair and trying to hold on to it. Saliva was disgustingly flowing from her mouth.

"Peter, I have to see this!" carter said as he pulled me into a small room.

There was nothing strange in the room. Except for something with a white sheet on it. And I noticed that this was something moving from under a sheet.

I was worried, and terror flowed into my heart. My body began to tremble on its own, and I said to carter quickly:

"What do I have to see, carter?"

"This is...".

He let out a scream of terror and jumped back to hit my back against the wall hard.

It was something—something impossible for me to forget all my life. Something you don't see even in your worst dreams and nightmares.

An old man turned into something like a giant fish.

His head, neck, and chest were normal. But both of his arms merged with the sides of his chest.

And both legs as well... They merged as if they had been close since birth.

And a man was sleeping on his stomach. And something disgusting... It's strange. Out of the back of an old man. Like a fin...

And I heard an old man moaning. After he turned into what looked like a giant human fish, an intermittent voice came out of his throat as if he were unable to speak.

"m... Alif... I... ".

Carter covered the old man and looked at me with pitiful eyes, saying:

"he's dying slowly; maybe we should take him to the beach!"

"As .... If... How it happened...".

"I don't know; his daughter Sarah saw a scene when she woke up in the morning next to her father from what... She was so terrified and frightened that she became... Crazy!! ".

She looked at the little girl, and there was a clear madness in her eyes and horror filling her from head to toe, carter added:

"Neighbors woke up to the sound of Sarah's screams, and when they came... Its existence is like this!".

I came out of a room with carter. As soon as I went out into the blue sky to breathe, I was very happy. I took a long breath as carter said:

"Something unbelievable and a real horror that hasn't started yet!".

He looked at carter with fear.

"I didn't understand? What do you mean?".

"This is the first case, peter. There are three other cases!! ".

Carter forced me to go with him to see the three strange cases of fishermen. The second case was after that of an old man... It's for a teenager. He is eighteen years old.

It was a very sophisticated case of illness or curse that afflicted him. He had leather fins protruding from his back, legs, and arms, indescribably adjacent to his body.

Current third she's a woman. It was similar to the two cases before it. But what interested me were the strange woman's teeth. As if it is a fish tooth, and scary is the shape of her head now. The first and second cases were of a head that still kept the hair on it.

However, ...

This is the case. A woman's hair disappeared, and she became bald and even... The size and shape of its head changed to become close to the shape of the fish's head.

The case of the last one, I don't know anything about. I vomited when i saw the fish's mirror. But from the exit of carter, who quickly told me:

"This is a very bad condition; he died of asphyxiation!".

"Man or woman?"

"It was a young man in his thirties. I asked his parents about him; they said that he stayed in his room for three nights and never came out of it, and when they noticed this matter, they opened the door of the room to find...".

"Turn into a fish!"

"Exactly, and he died of suffocation!"

"They can't breathe like us.".

"I think so; we're going to take them to the beach.".

Carter interrupted, saying:

"You don't intend to throw them into the seawater!"

"they're done, peter; there's a curse on this village; people turned into fish!"

And indeed, after a few moments, a blond-haired boy came running quickly towards carter, stood in front of him, panted, trying to gather his breath, and then said:

"Sir, there is... There's a strange corpse at the beach!".

Carter, a boy, and I ran outside the village towards the beach. We find a large gathering of the villagers standing, talking about something that fell on the sands.

"what's the matter?" said carter as he defended people for seeing the strange thing. And I'm with him.

I don't know how to describe how I felt at that time. But it was the strangest thing I've ever seen.

A corpse that cannot be described with the ugliest descriptions, words, and phrases.

It was half-upper... For a young girl with golden hair who was topless like a nymph.

And half inferior. For an octopus. Or squid, i don't know exactly what it is. But tens and tens of octopus legs extend from her belly to the end of her body.

Carter said:

"Oh my god, what is this thing?!"

One man with a light mustache said:

"Maybe it's a mermaid! Do you agree with me?! ".

One of the women of the village, who was fat as a barrel and one of the villagers most hated because of her fanaticism about her religion, said:

"This is a blessing from our lord, men; the lord blesses us with his blessings!!".

Carter shouted:

" Stop me from this nonsense; this is something that is not a gift from your god! This is something that should be we must bury him!".

Carter looked at all the men and women around him and shouted at them when he saw them looking at the being. With strange fascination! Like a thief who looks at a precious jewel

"What are you looking at?! Come on... Let's carry it for -- ".

A woman said:

"No, don't bury her... It's the lord's message to us!! ".

Since the arrival of the terrifying corpse, it's been three normal days... Like other days, but then things began to become... Strange.

Some children, especially infants, started crying all night annoyingly and for no logical reason to explain what they were afraid of exactly! Carter and I had gone to one of these cases.

Carter asked the baby crying on his mother's chest:

" Why are you crying, baby?! "

A child's crying grew more intense, but he said:

" She wants me to eat! ..."

Carter looked at me and then looked at the child and said,

" Who wants to eat you? "

The woman octopus."

My eyes widened as I heard these words. And then we walked out of the house, and we heard a baby crying inside. Carter said to me, looking at the stars shining in the darkness of the night:

" I've heard; what do you think?"

" This is not possible; we buried the strange corpse in a distant cemetery. Do not tell me that the dead come out at night!!"

Carter sighed to tell us:

" People turning into fish and a strange corpse on our shores. And now. Something scares the children of the village."

" I forgot something. What did you do for the fishermen, carter?! "

" He dropped them into the sea, and imagine what! They swam like little fish swim! "

I raised my eyebrows in astonishment and said,

" No new cases of fish turning have emerged, right? "

" True, but I don't know what tomorrow has in store for us. "

And I felt a hand placed on my right shoulder, and my body shivered, and I jumped away to see that it was Vander the madman, and he had a fire lantern in his hand while holding the white book that we saw in his hut. He said to us, amid our surprise, that he came to the village:

" I've heard of something that has landed on our shores: carter, a corpse, or something like that."

" Right, where have you been?! It's been three days since a corpse appeared. Any way... You--."

" Carter, do you know what this means? ... The arrival of a corpse."

Carter replied, furrowing his brow:

" I didn't understand. What do you mean?"

" it's a letter, carter... A message for a sample of it... From the great..."

" Fair enough... And... And what are we going to do? "

" We can't do anything about this; the great will come out soon... Maybe not in a liberal way. But we will become food for him... Our souls... He wants her. It's their only source of subsistence. "

Carter looked at me, and then i looked at him and then asked Vander:

" But you said they were immortal? "

" Correct... Immortal... That is... No, you won't understand anything very well. If they don't feed on human souls, they will go into a deep slumber. Do you understand this talk? "

I answered Vander:

" Yes... Understand... Now, what do we care about this? "

Vander said:

" I have to see a corpse... What did it look like? "

Carter said:

" half-topless girl... And it's the bottom half. Octopus..."

"Is she a god?" you added to carter's words.

Vander looked at us with skeptical eyes and then said to us,

Where did you bury a body?

Carter said:

In a cemetery far from a village.

" Come on... I want to see it!! "

" Vander! Do you understand what you are saying?! Is midnight time and..."

" I don't care about the time... I want to see a body right away."

Carter looked at me for help, but I didn't know what to say. There was an urgent curiosity in me. I want to look into that. So, the body of the...

I told carter:

" let's go with him. Come on... We won't be too late..."

And the three of us walked outside the village. Near the cemetery, far from a village, and while we were wandering at night, i had a mysterious feeling. A comfortable but uncomfortable feeling! I don't know how to describe it to you. You know when someone brings you a gift, and you know what a gift is. But there remains... That's the curious feeling that insists on you.

I knew a body was still there in a grave. And we went late at night. It's just a boring, silly trip.

However, ...

As soon as we got to the wooden cemetery fence, we realized that there was something wrong somewhere.

Carter quickly said:

" let's hide behind this tomb."

The three of us hid. Each one left a certain grave. Let's look at that scene. A scene with which it is hard to describe those feelings and feelings that you have, and you see this is an order

A group of village women. About twenty women. They dance naked around the body of the mysterious being. And they repeat rituals and words that are not understood but are annoying to everyone who hears them.

He was a beast crucified like Christ on his grave. While spinning around him in circles.

Carter whispered to me:

" what's this? "

" I don't know. Ask Vander."

But I only felt a strong blow on my head. A blow that lost consciousness and fell on the dust... And I heard carter's screams, and then everything was covered in darkness.

I woke up feeling a very strong pain all over my body. And I realize that there is blood coming down from my head to the right side of my face. But as soon as I noticed my situation...

The pain increased a lot, and I forgot my blood...

I was suspended. All of it, but crucified like a pool...

I looked down. I found it going around us. Oh my god, what happened?

" Peter! ... Are you okay? "

I looked to the right. I found carter crucified like me. Carter told me:

" don't try to move your hands. Or nails."

I looked at both hands. I found that the nails had been fixed there. And I squeezed my teeth hard while my heart melted from the terrible pain.

" Carter, what happened? "

" Vander... He betrayed us. "

" No, I didn't betray you."

Vander said it as he entered the circle. But it wasn't the Vander we knew... It was... It was something else entirely...

Blue skin. Fins fill his head from two sides, and a big fin is behind his back. And his fingers were blurred, like amphibious fingers.

Carter said:

" Oh my god."

A blue monster stepped forward to say:

" We will introduce you to our gods. The great cyberworth."

I quickly said:

" The what! Vander -- "

Here another object progresses: the creature that we found on our beaches. Octopus. The girl said, with her red eyes shining in darkness:

" Come on, my dear... He's calling us from the beach."

Vander nodded and shouted at the

" Come on, carry the sacrifices."

A sharp pain arose when the crucified wooden pole was moved onto it, and crowds began to move towards the village, led by Vander and that girl with octopus legs.

" Peter! Peter."

Carter was calling me while I was busy worrying about myself, and the horror was increasing as they approached a step. It's impossible... It is impossible. How can one woman carry a wooden column?? Does it require a pole of six men to carry it? Unless she is a non-human woman.

The horror started to flow inside my body, and sweat was pouring with running blood from my head. And both hands hurt because of the nails attached to them.

She shouted out loud:

" Vander! ‹ Vander... "

But he was far away. We got to our village. And i've seen houses of this height. The people of the village were looking at us with their eyes... Horror and fear. But they're not trying to save us! Why?? ...

We got to the beach of the village... I was pinned... In front of a beach and next to me, carter is screaming... Like a child about to take a needle.

Vander progressed. Or where that blue stranger is... And a loud sound to the extent that the drum of my left ear was torn by the sound of...

Silence...

You only hear the calm waves of the sea. Oh my god, save me. Please, save me...

A mass appeared from the middle of the sea. A black mass... In front of our eyes, me and carter.

All prostrated. And Vander and that girl... And even the people of the village who were looking from afar.

And a yellow light emerged from that black mass. Yellow light.

He blinded my eyes the moment he hit me.

And after you lost my sight, for seconds I heard carter's voice screaming from the horror he saw that night.

For the first time, I cried. I cried like a baby. He wants safety.

" Please, please "

I only felt the sticky messages holding my stomach and, with it, a pole that took it off from the sand of the beach.

" Please... "

I only felt like I had entered a tunnel—or a well. Quiet, sticky, and silent... And I kept screaming and screaming until my ropes cut off my voice.

Done.

Babylon Cat

There are many reasons and horror is one

You might be surprised by this phrase but wait until you hear the rest of the story

I know you won't believe me. Or believe my story But I am forced to reveal it but not for your sake ... But for mine

To get rid of that horror and those nightmares that attack me at night.

Everything happened. When they came.

Who were they you ask?

Gypsies... Of course.

They claimed to be coming from Babylon... To my city ... Karbala.

I used to live in a place outside the city called (the modern village) and it was a village like the rest of the neighboring villages

It has fields and farms for raising livestock k and pens for chickens and everything related to agriculture or animal husbandry.

I forgot to tell you by my name. My name is Ali Fadel. I know you don't care about my name as much as you care about my stories...

But I'm trying to be polite here. A s I write these words ...

And of course, out of general manners of telling you my name first, but I forgot, so pardon me ...

They came from Babylon as they claim.

They're strangers. In everything.

Clothes.

The Tattoos they draw on their bodies.

Even their animals were strange to me. Believe me when I say that most of the animals are black.

You might be surprised by this statement that I told you

But for God's sake. Tell me.

When was the last time you saw an animal in Black!!

Yes... You haven't? ... You've never seen a black rooster in your life.

Good That's what I meant.

Before I continue my story, I want to tell you about a habit rooted here. In my village.

When any tribe or Bedouins or group passes by us, I mean, here. They pass by our village to continue their way

There's a tradition followed here. And it's good hospitality

We are like any village. We welcome Bedouins, gypsies, and all the travelers who pass through our village.

So don't be surprised by this habit.

I know that these are customs that do not exist in the city.

But the situation is different here in the countryside...

Generally.

We welcomed them. With an open mind And I wish we didn't do that.

Everything was strange and suspicious about them... Those gypsies. But something caught my interest. To the extent that as I write these words in this dark room, I feel terrified.

And I try as much as I can not to look at the door

Maybe something will appear from under the door.

And I'm scared easily from everything. Even my shadow

That thing they the Gypsies brought with them ... It was a

Cat ... Yes... Just a black cat.

But it is from Babylon.

It was a huge cat. Strangely thick - haired. Yellow eyed ...

And the gypsies apparently...they respect it indescribably.

But...

They sanctify it!! ...

Yes.

They revere him like a

Goddess.

I ask God for forgiveness but it's the truth. Believe me, this is true. I'm not lying here.

They treated it the best

Even the soil that the cat walks on

They were.

Here I have to ask God for forgiveness.

They were kissing it... They kiss the dirt on which the cat walks!!

Anyway.

I met a Gypsy woman at dawn She was pale red head and called Kanasha. A strange name, but it doesn't matter.

Kanasha is the same age as me 19, once while we were attending a tomato field.

She was standing on a hill. While her red hair flies behind her neck due to the cold winds during the rise of the sun to the sky

I asked Kanasha about the cat:

"Why do you sanctify that black cat?"

Kanasha laughed:

"We don't sanctify it, we nurture it!"

"You sponsor it?! Why?? ".

Here Kanasha knelt down and took some dirt from the ground, saying:

"In order to avoid the wrath of our mother!"

"I don't understand what you mean?"

She threw dirt in the air, saying:

If our mother gets angry from us, we will become like this dust. We'll be blown by the wind."

That was the only conversation about this.

As far as I remember ...

Frankly, I try to collect my memories of those events.

But I don't want to.

I don't want to remember that horror.

One moment!

What was that?

Forget it.

I thought I saw a shadow moving under the door...

Anyhow... Let's finish this quickly.

Of course... Our village was surprised by the habits of the gypsies and their exaggerated actions towards this cat

One moment.

Let me tell you just one piece of information...

Namely...

This is the strangest cat I have ever seen in my life!!

Yes.

The strangest cat

How?

Listen to this, then.

When it looks at its prey ... Like roots or birds, I can almost swear.

If it's a rat or a bird.

They freeze in place Literally... They don't move and do not run away or try to hide

It's like a hypnotist.

And a second piece of information the cat moves very fast.

But sometimes... You see it somewhere. And when you blink ... You see, it disappeared from its place. By leaps and bounds...!

How so?... I don't know... No one knows?

And one of the times ... Kanasha told me that they keep several cat statues of different sizes and shapes. And they're all black.

And she also told me. That every gypsy... Sleep with a statue of these cats under their pillow. And if they don't... The gypsy will get sick and then on the third day They won't find a dead body, only white bones.

Generally, ...

I Forgot... One Thing.

Even the animals that the gypsies brought with them they get scared or terrified when they see the cat.

It's just like rats and birds. They freeze in place

And honestly Maybe you're thinking I'm exaggerating this. It's just an ordinary cat.

How can a normal cat ... Make a horse kneel to it?

Yes... As I heard.

One of the times ... When the sun was about to set.

I went to the stable. To give food to the horses.

And here I found that cat.

The horses were in a strange position. Where the right side is kneeling on the ground while the rest are in a

State of depression. Even their heads were arched towards the cat.

As if they were subject to Him... Or sanctifying it

Maybe you're asking me. Your usual question. Tell me about ... Dogs.

When I tell you the truth, you won't believe me.

Even dogs themselves ...

Run away from this cat!! ...

No other dog or animal dared to approach it.

I think you have it now. A complete picture of the beginning of the events of.

The what? The beginning of events?

Yes... My dear...

The real horror hasn't started yet.

Wait. Until I close this door.

I saw that the door opened by itself! Maybe the wind ...   Opened the door.

One moment... Let me close it and get back to you...

(The sound of the door closing and then locking)

Here you go. I couldn't find d anyone outside the door. And I don't know how the wind opened the door? But it's not our story.

Let me finish.

The horror started when...

The cat sneaked into Abu Hassan's house. Who doesn't know Abu Hassan's house?

Abu Hassan's house. Is a small   house built of fossilized clay like the village houses?

The father lives at home. And who honestly, I don't know his full name.

Because this is an old man. He was alive before I came to this world. So, all the guys are like me in a village

They call him A bu Hassan. Because we don't know his

Name.

And his wife um Hassan. An old woman like her husband

Of course... They have a son. And he is good. But Hassan was martyred in the Isis war in 2015 in Mosul seven years ago. May he rest in peace.

What's Known for this   couple is ... Their strong hatred for cats. For no reason

You know ...

Signs of aging. First... Animal Abuse.

Without a reason or even if there is a reason, they hit cats with stones or sometimes they even kill them with guns.

Quick information: Abu Hassan ow ns a rifle from the days of the Iraq and Kuwait wars because he was an army officer.

Generally.

When the Babylonian cat sneaked into Abu Hassan's house.

During the night and while everyone is asleep. We heard gunshots. To be exact the sound of five bullets.

In the morning

I woke up to the sound of screaming and wailing

I ran outside with my family. Let's check the situation

Outside.

Here I found.

All gypsies ... They wail and cry intensely... Gathered in the form of a circle and in the center of the circle ... On the soil of the ground... The body of that cat. The Babylonian cats.

The sounds of women screaming and crying of children. And the anger that glitters in the eyes of their men

And on the other side

The people of my village were laughing faintly as they looked at that laughable sight.

And whispering among themselves. That these gypsies have gone crazy.

And of course, it was a shocking sight for me

Very s hocking...

To see women taking off their veils and plucking their black hair and trying to tear their clothes as if the deceased is one of their relatives or family.

And not just a black cat ...

At night... I heard knocking on my door. The moon was shining.

I opened the door to see Kanasha standing and eyeliner was coming down from her red eyes from crying.

"kanasha, what is the matter?"

"I came to warn you, you have to run away quickly."

"Run?! Where to? And why? ".

"Run away, they'll summon him! "

"Summon? Who is it? What are you talking about?"

Here she said the strangest sentence I have ever heard:

"They will summon him from ... The Moon! ".

Kanasha quickly ran in front of me while I quietly closed the door of the house with proof in my head of the madness of these gypsies.

Early in the morning ...

I got out of my house. And I took a walk in a village as usual in the morning

But I was surprised that all the residents of the village were gathered around something.

I tried to shove myself f in the crowd.

To be surprised by the view in front of me

All the dawn prostrates on the ground... While they make strange sounds in an incomprehensible language.

And in the forefront of this kneeling crowd

A gypsy woman knelt. She is fat and the green tattoo covered both her hands.

She was kneeling ... While she addresses ...

Addresses the sky with words and sentences that are not understood...

She raises a yellow bowl above her head. She says:

"Forsaken... Oh master of destinies and the conqueror of universal entities. (Incomprehensible language). Statues ... The master of terror and horrors.... Dark Stringer ... (Understandable language) White hand ... Emartith ... Pluto... (Ununderstood language) ... (Incomprehensible language) (Understandable language) ... ".

Of course... The sounds of laughter rose from all sides Based on this blasphemy and polytheism in God

But in the next moment.

An old woman took. A knife from under her strange clothes. And tore her throat in front of everyone.

Sounds of screaming and screaming became louder. During the fall of the old woman's body.

But what really scared me They follow her. They didn't get up from their prostration. But they continued to recite her words and forbidden names.

While the people of my village are trying to save the old woman

A strong wind blew ... It's a storm of rage.

And the clouds started to gather at an unnatural speed. To block the sunlight from a village

And everyone looked at the sky.

The worshippers raised their heads towards the gray sky.

And there's a mysterious lightning. And shining from among the clouds By Almighty God,

I have seen something moving from among the clouds...

I swear by God

I saw something. A black shadow moving among the clouds while the lightning is striking

And the situation continued like this

And the winds got stronger and forced everyone to enter their homes.

And here I don't know what happened outside.

But I looked out a window. It was a house that had one window.

I looked through it.

And I saw what I saw...

Something cam e down from the sky... Something like black threads ...

And we heard a noise outside. And loud screams.

And here, I swear to God

I heard a trumpet

A trumpet so loud that ... Everyone's ears have been torn My father's and mother's heads have exploded in front of me. In a split moment.

Yes, it exploded like balloons when you pierce it with a needle.

I screamed in horror and shock and ran outside....

To be surprised by a thick fog ... There is no explanation for it.

Fog you don't see anything except from a close distance

I heard the screams of women mixed with the crying of children and the voices of men screaming for help.

And I saw them.

I saw them rise to the top. Everything rises up in the fog.

The mud village houses.

Animals.

The people of the village

They are slowly rising to the sky.

And there are what looks like threads everywhere. Black threads descending from the sky from among the c louds.

And in the next moment...

I saw even the grains of sand that I am standing on started to rise Around me.

Everything was flying lightly and quietly.

Chaos is everywhere.

And horror around me It spins like a wheel...

I fell on the ground And I grabbed the hair on my head and started screaming. I scream while holding the hair on my head with both hands.

Calling on my mother on my father ... On God On my friends on the people of my village ... For everything.

I can't bear all this horror.

I can' t stand all this madness.

And here. At this moment... I saw it... Who is it? ... The Moon... Of course.

The clouds emptied for a moment and I saw it ...

It was red as the color of blood.

Big as the size of the earth.

Shining as a precious essence.

I got up from the ground ... And I walked with confident steps Near the Moon... Yes... That's what I want... I want the moon ...

I love it. I love it ... I can't live without it...

The Moon...

At this moment I felt a hand being placed on my shoulder.

I turned to see Kanasha wearing a necklace and said:

"Close your eyes! And never open it."

"Ha, what?"

"Don't open your eyes no matter what!"

I wore a necklace and closed my eyes. And of course. I don't need to tell you ab out the horror I heard.

Sounds of women screaming.

Crying babies.

Sounds of animals.

Howling dogs.

Chicken sounds

The screams of men.

The sounds of houses while they are being destroyed

I heard all this with my eyes closed. A street with horror that breaks my heart

In the morning I woke up.

I was lying on the soil I opened my eyes to see a clear sky And I don't know where I am.

But I was in a place far from my village.

It took me a while to find my village.

And here is the last horror scene I saw before I ran away from my village for once and for all...

I found all the inhabitants of the villages and they merged in the form of a giant ball of legs, feet, arms and hands. And in the midst of all this ... Their faces were screaming with horror that their minds could not comprehend.

So much so that their eyes have become protruding white and their mouths open in a screaming posture like a witness to horror that no human being can bear at all.

This is my story and you have the right to believe it or not

If you see a black cat ... Don't kill it or throw a stone at it but let it leave you in peace and safety.

END.